Metaphysics: A Very Short Introduction

VERY SHORT INTRODUCTIONS are for anyone wanting a stimulating and accessible way into a new subject. They are written by experts, and have been translated into more than 45 different languages.

The series began in 1995, and now covers a wide variety of topics in every discipline. The VSI library now contains over 500 volumes—a Very Short Introduction to everything from Psychology and Philosophy of Science to American History and Relativity—and continues to grow in every subject area.

Titles in the series include the following:

Stephen Mumford

METAPHYSICS

A Very Short Introduction

OXFORD
UNIVERSITY PRESS

OXFORD
UNIVERSITY PRESS

Great Clarendon Street, Oxford OX2 6DP,
United Kingdom

Oxford University Press is a department of the University of Oxford.
It furthers the University's objective of excellence in research, scholarship,
and education by publishing worldwide. Oxford is a registered trade mark of
Oxford University Press in the UK and in certain other countries

British Library Cataloguing in Publication Data
Data available

Library of Congress Cataloging in Publication Data
Data available

ISBN 978-0-19-965712-4

Printed and bound by CPI Group (UK) Ltd, Croydon, CR0 4YY

Contents

Acknowledgements

I am grateful to Andrea Keegan for showing confidence in this book and my writing of it. I use an example from Phil Dowe in Chapter 9 that I heard in a talk he gave. I am also grateful to Rani Lill Anjum with whom I have worked on causation and to Roger Kerry for explaining the significance of randomized controlled trials. I am grateful to Rani Lill Anjum a second time for having commented on a first draft as did Ruth Groff. I thank my teachers of metaphysics and also my students, who have given me ample opportunity to think about the topics discussed here.

List of illustrations

What is an introduction?

Metaphysics is one of the traditional four main branches of philosophy, alongside ethics, logic, and epistemology. It is an ancient subject but one that continues to arouse curiosity. It holds an attraction for many who have only a basic inkling of what it is but are keen to know more.

For some, it is associated with the mystical or religious. For others, it is known through the metaphysical poets who talk of love and spirituality. This book will aim to introduce the uninitiated to how metaphysics is understood and practised by philosophers. Many introductions to the topic begin with a consideration of what metaphysics is and how its truths can be known. But this itself is one of the most difficult and contentious questions, and the reader could quickly become bogged down and lose interest. This book is therefore written back to front. The question of what metaphysics is and how it is justified will be left to the very last. The best way to understand an activity is often through doing it rather than theorizing about it. In that case, we start by doing some metaphysics: considering some seemingly simple little questions but which concern the fundamental nature of reality.

We will go through a variety of issues with only a few technical concepts and terms. By the end, there should be a fair grasp of the problems around substance, properties, changes, causes, possibilities, time, personal identity, nothingness, and emergence. It is hoped that the book will not intimidate its readers in a way that many philosophy books – particularly in metaphysics – can.

Often, the ideas, concepts, and questions of metaphysics sound easy – childish even. What are objects? Do colours and shapes have some form of existence? What is it for one thing to cause another rather than just being associated with it? What is possible? Does time pass? Do absences, holes, lackings, and nothingnesses have any form of positive existence at all? To some, these seem like silly questions, but for others they are at the core of what philosophy is all about. And those who see it that way often get a sense that the issues these questions raise are the most fundamental and profound about which humans can think. Metaphysics is the subject among all others that inspires the sense of wonder in us, and for that reason some think that doing metaphysics is the most valuable use we could make of our time.

If you have made it this far, perhaps metaphysics has already captured your imagination and your curiosity. In that case, we should begin forthwith on our little tour of the metaphysical furniture of the world. But where to begin? Philosophers never really know. The things they worry about are often interconnected. To understand one issue, you need first to understand another. Yet we have to say the same about the second issue as well: to understand it, you need to understand a third, and so on. And this seems to be true no matter where we start. Sometimes an understanding of the world comes only by grasping the whole, which makes it hard to explain the problems of philosophy in a neat sequence, as books must inevitably try to do. Where we begin is thus to an extent arbitrary.

Chapter 1
What is a table?

When I look at the world around me, I see that I am surrounded by all sorts of things. I see a table and two chairs, buildings, an aeroplane, a box of paper clips, pens, a dog, people, and a wide variety of other kinds of things. But this is a book about metaphysics, and in metaphysics we are concerned with the nature of things in very general terms. I am tempted to say, as a metaphysician, that all of these things I have listed are particular things, or groups or kinds of them. The notion of a particular is very important to us. I want to know that the pen on the table is my particular one rather than someone else's, or that the woman in the room really is my wife rather than her identical twin sister. To understand the importance of these issues, we need to probe them more deeply.

In front of me stands a table that I can see, feel, and hear if I rap my knuckles on it. I have no doubt that it – the table – exists. But now I will start the philosophical questions. What is this thing? What is the nature of its existence? Is the table something I know through experience or do my senses reveal to me something else? After all, when I look at it, I see its colour: the brownness of the wood. And when I feel it, I feel its hardness. Brownness, hardness, four-leggedness, and so on, are the qualities or properties of the table. One might then be tempted to say that I do not know the table itself but only its properties. Does that then mean that the table is an underlying something about which I know nothing? Its properties seem wrapped around it and impossible to strip away.

What goes for tables, goes for other particular things too. There is nothing special in the choice of a table as my example. In the cases of coins, motor cars, books, cats, and trees, I know them only through knowing their qualities. I see their shape, their colour, I can feel their texture, smell their fragrance, and so on. The nature of these properties of things – redness, roundness, hardness, smelliness, and so on – will be the topic of the next chapter. But we really cannot avoid mentioning properties as soon as we mention the particulars to which they attach.

The more things change, the more they stay the same

Now why would I suggest that the table is something other than the brownness, hardness, and four-leggedness that I can see in front of me? One reason is that I could imagine these properties changing while the table remains the same particular that it was. I could paint the table white, for instance, because it fits in better with the decor of my office. If I did that, then it would still be one and the same table, it would simply have changed its appearance. Something will have changed, while something has remained the same.

In philosophy, we see that all sorts of confusion can reign if we speak loosely of it being the *same* table, so we employ an important distinction. We can say that something has changed *qualitatively* even though it has remained *numerically* the same. So the table can be different in its qualities – it was brown and now it is white – but it remains one and the same thing. The table that was brown is now the table that is white. Imagine if a visitor comes into my room and asks what's happened to my old brown table. It's perfectly acceptable for me to respond that it's still here: it's just that they didn't recognize it because I had painted it. Being one and the same, despite such changes in qualities, is what we mean by *numerical* sameness (the topic of change will be explored more in Chapter 4).

It is this consideration that leads me to think that the table itself cannot be the same thing as its properties. At least some of them could change and yet it would still be the same table. So when I look at and feel the properties of the table, I am observing just that – its properties – and not the table itself. But what, then, is the table, if it is not its properties?

Here is a suggestion. The table is something that underlies the properties and holds them all together in one place. It is something I cannot see or touch, because all I experience is a thing's properties, but I know it is there through my rational thinking. When I move the table across the room, for instance, all of its properties move with it. They are clustered together in a semi-permanent way. It is not as if the brownness and hardness of the table can move but the four-leggedness can get left behind. I say that the properties are clustered only *semi*-permanently, though. As we have seen, some properties can be shed from the cluster and new ones take their place, so we cannot be absolutely strict and say that the properties are bound together inseparably. The brownness can be shed and replaced by whiteness.

Such a view of particulars may be best understood through the metaphor of a pin cushion that is used to hold pins together in one place. The pins represent the properties of an object and the cushion represents the particular itself. Some call this a *substratum* view of particulars, where the pin cushion is the substratum that underlies all the properties on view. One pin stands for the brownness of the table, another stands for its hardness, and a third stands for its weight, another its height, and so on for every single property the table has. And if we could strip these away – mentally, through a process of abstraction – we would come to understand that the thing itself is separate from

5

them and is that in which they all inhere. Of course, when you remove all the pins from a real pin cushion, you are still left with something that you can see and touch. But remember that our metaphorical pin cushion, when all its pins have been removed, is a particular that has been stripped of all its properties so that we can think of what the table itself is. And without properties, it couldn't therefore look or feel like anything.

Consider, for instance, a cat. We can think of it without its blackness; for that is a property and we want to know what the thing is that underlies all its properties. But removing its blackness isn't like skinning a cat. As well as removing its colour, we also have to take away its shape, as that is just another property like the rest, and so is its four-leggedness, smelliness, and furriness. Take all those away and we could well wonder what this underlying substratum really is. It would have to be invisible. It would have no length, breadth, or height, and no colour or solidity. There would be a bareness to it that may really make us start to wonder whether we have anything at all.

Philosophers are notorious for working out all the implications of an idea. But they don't necessarily always accept those implications. Sometimes a consequence is so ridiculous that it can be taken as good grounds for rejecting the initial supposition. Such a counterintuitive consequence will have reduced the supposition from which it sprang to absurdity. Perhaps we can say that's happened in this case. It was suggested that the particular had to be something other than its properties. But once we started to abstract away the properties of the cat from the cat itself, we realized that it would leave hardly anything. Our substratum-cat seems to be nothing at all. It has no weight, no colour, no extension in space, and so on. And this starts to look like a non-thing. Isn't it the case that everything that exists has properties? It is not as if 'bare' particulars could exist and that some of them were just fortunate enough to accidentally acquire properties. Certainly every physical thing that ever has and ever

6

will exist has some shape or weight or feature. And to talk as if the thing can in some way exist independently of those properties was perhaps the mistake that led us to absurdity.

Bundles of properties

Let us, in that case, consider a different approach. If there can be no 'bare' particulars, existing without having properties, then we might want to think again of the cluster or bundle of properties with which we began. When in our minds we stripped away those properties, in a process of abstraction, the fear was that we were left with nothing at all. So shouldn't we then just countenance the possibility that there is nothing more to a particular than that bundle of properties? If there really is no remainder once all the properties have been removed, then we know that our particular cannot be more than them. The bundle view is that particulars can be accounted for in terms only of properties. How plausible is this view?

There are a couple of problems associated with it, which come from the problem of change that we already discussed. If a thing were just a collection of properties, it couldn't survive any change. If one property were lost and another gained, we would have a different collection: for I am assuming that what makes a collection the same thing at different times is that it is composed of the same component things. Consequently, two collections are different if the things collected within them are different. And clearly, the particulars that interest us change all the time while remaining (numerically) the same. A cat changes its shape frequently. Sometimes it is lying out flat, other times it is rolled up in a ball, and then it might be running around, changing its shape continuously. How can the cat be just a collection of properties when they change all the time?

It may be possible to answer this objection, though. Perhaps we should think of a thing as a series of bundles of properties, united by a degree of continuity. So while the table can be changed and painted white, it keeps roughly the same weight, height, and physical position. I am assuming the physical position of an object is one of its properties, and clearly it is a pretty important one in this context. I am confident the white table is the same thing as the previous brown table in no small part because I find it in the same room. And if it has moved, I expect that it did so gradually by passing through a series of locations between where it started out and where it ended up. While the cat changes shape rapidly, it keeps the same colour, furriness, smell, and, importantly, it is in the same place; or if it has changed its position, it has done so through a series of locations. We could say, therefore, that while the bundles of properties come and go, a particular thing is a succession of such bundles with an appropriate continuity running throughout.

There are a number of other difficulties to be faced, but before going on to consider one of them, it is worth mentioning what might be a big advantage of this bundle view. The first account we considered was one in which particulars were underlying substrata that held the properties of a thing together. To account for particular objects such as a table, a chair, a dog, and a tree, we had two kinds of ingredients. We had a thing's properties and its substratum. But with this new bundle theory, it seems that we need only one kind of thing. We just have the properties and, when they come in a bundle or a continuous sequence of such bundles, we say that we thereby have a particular object. So where we previously needed two elements, we now have only one. Another way of looking at this is to say that the notion of substratum has been reduced away entirely in other terms. Objects would just be nothing more than bundles of properties, appropriately arranged.

The second theory is thus a simpler one in so far as it invokes fewer kinds of entity. The unknowable formless substratum seemed to give us nothing extra: if the bundle theory is correct, then the substratum is dispensable. Now there is no particular reason why a simpler and more economical theory is more likely to be true than a complex and uneconomical one, but philosophers prefer the simple ones. Certainly, there seems no reason to tolerate redundancy in one's theory of the world because any redundant elements are clearly not needed for the account to work. They serve no purpose.

Identical twins

The bundle theory looks simpler than a substratum view, therefore. But is it too simple? Would it have enough resources to deliver all we want of a particular thing? There is one consideration that suggests not. A particular, we are told by this theory, is just a collection of properties. A snooker ball, for instance, is just a bundle of the properties red, spherical, shiny, 52.5 millimetres in diameter, and so on. The problem for the theory, however, is that there could be another object with exactly those properties. Indeed, for the game of snooker to be fair, there should be many red balls with those same properties: they are standardized. The theory has a difficulty here, however. It tells us that a particular just is the bundle. But then, if we have the same bundle, it implies that we have the same object. In other words, there could not, on this theory, be more than one object that is the same bundle of properties.

It might be said that this objection is a mere technicality that doesn't really matter. Couldn't it just be that, as a matter of fact, two distinct objects never really do share all the same properties? Even tables that are mass-manufactured will have some very slight difference in weight, colour, or even just the pattern of fine, microscopic scratches on the surface. Our snooker balls need only be close enough in their properties for the game to be playable fairly so they too can have some slight differences. This response misses the point of a philosophical theory, however. This was supposed to be an account of what it is

9

to be a particular thing. The truth of that theory should not have to rely on luck working out for it, such that every particular thing just happens to be a different bundle. It does seem at least a possibility that two things could share all their properties. And if, as the theory states, particulars are only and nothing more than bundles of properties, then it is inconsistent with that possibility. Two particulars with the same properties collapse into one.

There are two possible ways out for the bundle theorist but both have problems. The first apparent solution is to say that there is a reason in principle why two particulars could not share all their properties. If one allows relational properties, then these arguably must differ because they allow spatiotemporal location to come into the equation. The following example illustrates what is meant by a relational property. Even if all the red snooker balls are indistinguishable when you inspect them, perhaps one is just 20 centimetres from the bottom-right pocket of the snooker table, while the other is 30 centimetres from it. One ball has the relational property of being 20 centimetres from the pocket, while the other has the relational property of being 30 centimetres from the same pocket. Assuming no two entirely distinct particulars can occupy the same space at the same time, then it seems that all things will bear a unique set of relational properties.

Here is the problem with this proposal. There is no guarantee that distinct things really will have different relational properties unless we reintroduce particulars into our metaphysics. This is why. Should we think of position in space (and time) as an absolute or relative matter? If it were absolute, it would suggest that there is some kind of particularity to spatial positions. A position would be a particular. The notion of a particular – one that is not defined as a bundle of qualities – will have come back into the theory. That's no good because we were looking to eliminate particulars in terms of bundles of properties.

So do we instead define spatial positions in relation to each other? The problem with doing so is that there is at least the possibility that the space of a universe has a line of symmetry; and thus places in corresponding positions either side of the line of symmetry would bear an identical set of relations to all the other places within the whole of that space. If we then position two of our snooker balls at those corresponding points within our symmetrical universe, then it remains a theoretical possibility that two distinct particulars nevertheless are identical in all their non-relational and relational properties. (This sounds a bit complicated, but Figure 1 shows what's meant.) On the bundle theory, they again collapse into each other.

This is a complicated argument. A short summary might help. We tried to separate indistinguishable particulars on the basis of them having different locations. But either those locations are themselves particulars, in which case we have not succeeded in eliminating particulars, or locations are just distinguished by their relations to each other. And in the latter case, the possibility of a symmetrical structure means that we could have

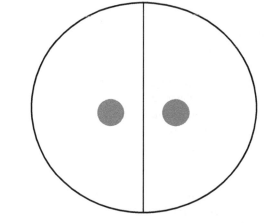

1. **A symmetrical universe**

two particulars that were not distinguishable even on the basis of location.

What we just had was a proposed first way for the bundle theorist to avoid the implication that particulars with all the same properties collapse into one. As that didn't seem to work, here is a second proposal. The objection, that the theory entails bundles with all the same properties must be one and the same, strikes only if the properties are to be understood in a certain way: as nothing like particulars. But there are other conceptions, as we will see in Chapter 2. Perhaps those properties are particularized in some way. Hence, the red in this bundle might be a different thing or instance from the red in another bundle. There might then be the possibility that there are distinct particulars with all the same properties. They consist of the same types of property but different instances of them. Isn't this what we think of all the red snooker balls? The red of this ball is not the same as the red of that ball. They are two different instances of red.

But there is again a problem with this apparent solution. We have saved the bundle theory but at a cost. An advantage of the bundle theory, it was noted, was that it accounted for particulars entirely in terms of properties. Particularity was reduced away in terms of properties. But it now seems that we are able to salvage the bundle theory from the objection that two identical bundles would collapse into one only if we understand properties in some way as particulars. We spoke of having two distinct instances of red and a property instance looks like some kind of particular. So to make our bundles behave more like the particulars that we take objects to be, we have had to make our properties like particulars. Particularity has managed to sneak back into the theory.

There are countless mistakes that we may have made along the way. But it looks like we might be forced to conclude that particularity is an irreducible feature of reality, for there could, in theory, be two distinct particulars whose distinctness did not consist in them having different properties.

So what, then, is a table? After the considerations in this chapter, it seems that we have to say it is a particular that bears certain properties but is not identical with, nor reducible to, those properties. The table was chosen arbitrarily as the object we examined, and it thus seems safe to generalize from it. We should then give the same answer for any other object.

The properties of particulars have been mentioned throughout this chapter. We need next to consider what these things are supposed to be, if indeed they are things at all. We move on, therefore, to this topic.

Chapter 2
What is a circle?

The opening question of this chapter is very simple to ask. What is a circle? You would have thought that in all the centuries of human civilization, we would have answered it by now. And there is at least one very clear and simple answer, which is provided by geometry. Mathematicians have a precise definition of a circle. But we should put aside that definition for now because it is not quite the type of answer that interests us.

Around us are various circular things: a coin, a wheel, the circumference of a ball, the rim of a cup, a line-drawing on a sheet of paper. There are various individual circles here, appearing at different places and times. There seems to be a something in common to all instances. What is common to them and the other things on the list is what we call circularity. We give this feature a name and treat it as if it is a single kind of entity. The same feature can be found in lots of different places and objects. Some speak of circularity as being a *One* that runs through *Many*. In all these many different particulars, the one circularity is to be found.

Going round in circles

There seems to be something strange about this thing circularity, if it really is a thing at all. Usually when one thinks of things, they are objects: particular objects such as tables, chairs, motor cars, buildings, trees, pens, and so on. Choose one such thing at random: a particular pen. This pen may sit on a particular desk in a particular house. It will have had a beginning in existence and a particular history. Now if this pen is on a particular desk, we know that it is nowhere else. And if a certain person owns the pen, we know that no one else does. Of course, a group of people may go into partnership to buy a pen jointly but, again, if that partnership owns the pen, then no one else does. The partners perhaps own a fraction of the pen each.

Sheep, tables, and pens are, then, particular objects. We can also speak of *a* circle, as if it is a particular thing. But *circularity* has a very different kind of nature. Unlike the case of the pen, the fact that circularity appears in one place or time does not stop it appearing at other places and times. And at all those places it appears, it is *wholly present*. This is different from the case of the pen. It being wholly owned by one person stops it being owned by another, whereas one thing being circular does not stop other things being circular. And when the pen is co-owned, each of the owners owns only part of the pen. But if a number of things are circular, each is wholly circular. It is not as if circularity has to be shared out in portions, such that if exactly two things had it, for instance, each would be semi-circular. That would be absurd because then neither of those things would be circular after all. This is what is meant by speaking of circularity being wholly present in all of its instances and it being a One thing that runs through Many others.

This may all seem like a confusing tangle, so let us try to straighten things out. One view is that there are two basic kinds of entity: particulars and their properties. Tables, chairs, and sheep are examples of particulars and they seem present only at one location at a time. Circularity is an example of a property: a feature or quality of a particular. The fact that a property appears in one place, in its entirety, puts no limit on it appearing elsewhere at other places and times. Because of this feature, some like to call properties *universals* – they can be at any place or time – though really this term is best used for one particular theory of what a property is. Other examples of properties are redness, squareness, being hairy, soluble, explosive, tall, and so on.

Related matters

There is much to be said metaphysically about such properties: about their nature and existence. But first, it should be noted that a distinction is usually made between properties and *relations*, and many of the same issues are found in the case of relations.

Alan is taller than his eldest son, Bobby. We can think of this as there being a relation of *taller than*, which Alan holds to Bobby. And there are many other instances of *taller than*, all over the place. Bobby is taller than his sister Clarissa, who is in turn taller than her dog Dougal. And the Empire State Building is taller than the Chrysler building. Again, it is arguable that this relation of being *taller than* is wholly present in each of its instances. Perhaps even more so than in the case of properties, it seems clear that it is the very same thing that appears in both the case of Alan being taller than Bobby and Bobby being taller than Clarissa. When we say one thing is taller than another, it seems that in every case we mean the same thing.

Let us now return to the case of properties, for we have all we need here to proceed to some of the really deep philosophical issues. Suppose someone were to gather every circular thing in the world, or every red thing, or every one-hundred-sided thing. No doubt this is a practical impossibility, but it is worth entertaining just as a thought experiment. Suppose they were then to crush all the circular things, or whatever the example is, until they were destroyed or at least no longer circular. Would they thereby have destroyed circularity? Arguably not. At best, they have destroyed all the instances of it. But can we say that circularity nevertheless exists? If so, where or when does it exist?

Metaphysics

Plato's heaven

Plato, one of the greatest philosophers of all, had an answer to this. At first, it sounds too fanciful, but reflection may dispel the feeling. Metaphysics often works like that. Plato didn't think you could destroy circularity. He thought that the instances of it with which we are acquainted are all imperfect copies of the true circularity. Every circular thing existing in the physical world will be defective in its circularity, to at least some degree, no matter how small. The geometrical definition of a circle is relevant here. Plato thought that only the mathematician was properly acquainted with a perfect circle, in which every point on the circumference was exactly the same distance from the centre. But all the circles we see in the world around us will have some slight deviation from this perfect or ideal circle. Now here is the fanciful part. Plato thought that the perfect circle existed in a heavenly, transcendent world: above and beyond the physical world of everyday objects that we inhabit. This heavenly realm would contain all the true versions of all the properties and relations too.

We need to take a pause at this point because the existence of a so-called *Platonic* realm where properties such as circularity, redness, hairiness, and relations such as *taller than* exist is pretty striking. This realm is not something we could ever see with our eyes or interact with physically. It has to be contemplated and understood through pure intellect, according to Plato. The idea appeals to the thought that there is more to the world than that which we humans have created.

Consider, for instance, the fact that 2 + 2 = 4. Wouldn't this still be true even if no one had ever thought about it, or even if no humans had ever existed? Suppose the universe had been barren, filled only with lifeless rocks. 2 + 2 rocks would still equal 4 rocks, even if no one would have been around to think of it or articulate it. In that case, there should be some appeal in Platonism because it seems that some things are too great and too perfect for our mundane and everyday world and thought.

Platonism is a very strong form of realism about properties. For Plato, they were more real than their imperfect copies that we ordinarily encounter. Only the Platonic circle was a perfect circle. All the rest are flawed. He called these perfect versions of properties *Forms*, and he thought they were the most real things of all. We knew they existed through our intellectual grasp alone, so we didn't have to worry about whether our senses misled us.

Not everyone likes the idea of Platonism. This may not be just a matter of personal preference. A Platonist divides existence into two realms: the one we inhabit and the heavenly one where properties exist. But whenever we divide something into two realms, we have to tell a story about how they relate and that often gets complicated. That problem afflicts this account. What is the relation supposed to be between the perfect Form of a circle and the individual circles that we see around us? Plato tried many times to answer this question, but without complete success. One circle exists in a heavenly realm, outside space and time. The other circles all exist imperfectly in space and time. So how can they possibly relate to the Form? Can they resemble the Platonic circle when they are so different in their natures?

There is a major difficulty for any such proposal. Suppose we wanted to say something like this: the worldly circles *resemble* the perfect Form of a circle. Resemblance is a relation. But a relation, it will be recalled, is also something that a Platonist thinks belongs in their heavenly realm. There would be a Form of resemblance, therefore. We would then have to answer the same question again: how does the *Form of resemblance* relate to the actual resemblance (between the worldly circle and the Form of a circle)? If we give the same answer – that it resembles it – we will have made no further progress. We will have embarked on what philosophers call an *infinite regress*. There will be a never-ending series of resemblances, and this would indicate that the original answer is no good: we never should try to say that the instances *relate* to the Form.

Platonism, however, is not the only option we have, so we need not despair if we think the theory looks doomed. There are two other main options. The first is an anti-realism about properties, certainly conceived of as universals. This needs explaining.

The starting point was an assumption that there are two basic kinds of thing in the world: particulars and properties. But not everyone accepts this. One reason for rejecting the division into two is precisely that they would need to be brought together in some way. We would have to get the roundness and the greenness, as properties, united with the physical things in the world, such as an apple. But that is when we have to start speaking of the apple instantiating those two properties, or some such account. Suppose, instead, we said that there was only one kind of thing. What if we said that everything in the world was a particular? (This is the opposite of the bundle theory of particulars considered in Chapter 1, which says that everything is a property.)

There is an attraction to this *particulars-only* view. I know that tables and chairs exist, and balls and screw-top jars, trees, pencils, coins, and all sorts of things. But I am slightly less sure about the idea of *circularity* being a *thing* that exists in the same way that a coin does. When the case for circularity was made earlier, it needed some work to make it sound plausible. But surely it doesn't take any work at all to persuade someone that all these different particulars are real.

It's all just words

What, then, do we say about the so-called properties? The view that everything is a particular is sometimes called *nominalism*, which means *name*-ism. The idea is that circularity is just a name – just a word – that we use to describe groups of particular objects. There are varieties of this theory, but one is that the name is applied to groups of particulars that resemble each other. Hence, there are particulars – a ball, a coin, a screw-top lid, a wheel, and so on – and circularity is just a name for the way in which these things resemble each other. Circularity itself is no thing. It has no existence or reality. Every single thing is a particular.

But nominalism has its own problems. It can be asked in what way the group of objects resemble each other. Suppose the group of things offered as examples – the coin, wheel, and jar lid, and so on – as well as all being circular were also all brown in colour. In that case, there seems to be more than one way or respect in which they resemble. Circularity cannot just be a resemblance between the things, therefore, for it seems it must be one individual resemblance in a certain respect.

This is potentially very damaging. It seems we have to appeal not just to the particular things but also to *ways* or *respects* in which they resemble; and a way or respect sounds like a property by another name. Our attempt to do away with properties and have only particulars looks to have run aground very quickly, therefore.

That's not all. Here is another problem. We said that groups of particulars resembled each other, and this was all a property consisted in. But, again, what is this resemblance thing? It sounds like a relation: a universal that apparently holds between all the particulars in the group. It seems, therefore, that we are again appealing to a universal – a relation in this case. Can we avoid doing so?

Suppose we said that resemblance was not a universal or Platonic Form. Like everything else according to nominalism, it is a particular. There would then have to be a particular resemblance that held between a pair of objects; but there would also be another particular resemblance that held between a further pair of objects. In what way are those two particular resemblances both resemblances? Again, resemblance cannot be a real relation. So it seems that we have to say that these two resemblances resemble each other. And then we need an account of that further resemblance. Again, this looks like an infinite regress in the offing.

This problem afflicts another view that is worth mentioning. It might be thought of as a variety of nominalism but also stands apart from it. The idea is that while the world is made up of particulars only, these particulars should be thought of not as particular objects but as particular qualities. This is a rejection of the view of properties as a genuine One running through Many. Rather, this redness is an entirely distinct thing to that other redness. Various patches of red can be found all over the place, just as there can be various circles. These particular attributes should be thought of as entirely separate existences from each other. The redness of one snooker ball is, after all, separate from the redness of another. One could exist even if the other didn't.

The technical term for these particularized qualities is *tropes*. But the same kind of difficulty arises for them. In virtue of what are all these tropes *red* tropes, for instance? What gives them their red nature? One may just say that it is a primitive fact about them that permits no further explanation. But that then starts to look like a realism about properties after all. Or one might say that they are all red because they resemble each other. But we have already seen the difficulties resemblance gets us into. Are there resemblance tropes? And do they resemble each other?

Back down to earth

Is there an alternative to Platonism and nominalism? We have seen the difficulties of both and might wonder whether there is a third way. Fortunately, there is. One of the most famous images in

What is a circle?

2. **Detail of** *The School of Athens*, **1510, by Raphael**

the history of philosophy is of the School of Athens painted by
Raphael (Figure 2). In the centre, Plato and Aristotle debate. Plato
is seen pointing up to the heavens. All that really matters is up
there. But Aristotle has a different view. He gestures down to
earth. No, he is insisting, it is all down here.

This Aristotelian view is one to consider. Plato's theory was described as a realism about properties but it is not the only form that such realism could take. The worry about it concerned its transcendent nature: properties residing in the Platonic heaven. But perhaps the properties could be real and exist down here, in the regular world of which we feel part. Such was Aristotle's view, which we can call an immanent realism, because properties are here with us. Circularity would be a real feature of the world but exist only in its instances: in circular things. One would have to accept that some such circles were imperfect. Perhaps that means that only imperfect circularity is a real property. Why not accept that? The mathematician's circle is really nothing more than a stipulated definition of something, which doesn't mean that it thereby exists. To exist, on this view, is for something to be it; and if nothing is perfectly circular, mathematically defined, then perfect circularity is not a property of our world.

But what of the point that if I crush every circular object, I cannot thereby have destroyed circularity? It doesn't seem that properties can go out of existence or come into it. Although this point may tempt one towards Platonism, there is another response. Suppose I say that a property exists in nothing more than its instances, but I mean in all the instances that ever have and ever will be? We can treat all times as equal rather than privileging the present. So if something somewhere is circular, be it only once, at any time, then that property exists and is real.

This doesn't end the matter. We still need to consider what it is to be an instance, and whether there are any tricky instantiation relations lurking around to thwart our theory. But we have seen that there is a possible position in which properties and relations can be understood as real but also down to earth. Undoubtedly, this view would need more development and defence, but it looks worth a try.

Chapter 3
Are wholes just sums of parts?

So many things in the world around us are complex rather than simple. A mobile phone, for instance, has many small parts that have all been assembled in a very specific way to make a complex but functioning whole. If I dissect a rat, I find that inside it are all sorts of wet and slimy parts. From what I know of biology, they would all have played a part in keeping the rat alive and active. Sometimes an object looks pretty simple from the outside, like an orange fruit, and then when I cut into it, I find that it also has parts under its skin. When we say in metaphysics that an object is complex, we usually mean just that it has parts. But there is a question to consider of whether those complex wholes are nothing more than sums of parts arranged in a specific way. This question turns out to be important, as we will see shortly. First, however, we should say a little more about complexity.

We may think something like the following. Many things are complex but at least some are absolutely simple: by which we mean that they have no parts. The existence of simples is questionable, however. We have in the past thought some things to be simple – atoms, for instance – that turned out to be complex. They were split and found to have smaller particles inside them. And some of these have in turn been found to have parts. This leaves us in a difficult position in respect of what can be known. The problem is that while we can know something to be complex, we cannot know it to be simple. We can see that something has parts; but if we don't see parts, we cannot be sure that they are not hidden or too small for us to see. And in that case, how do we know that anything is truly simple? We may just falsely believe that something is.

Parts all the way down

Must there be any simples at all? We often see parts within parts: in a motor car engine, for instance. Why shouldn't we assume that this pattern goes on forever and that there are always parts within parts?

Sometimes there is an insistence that all these parts within parts must end somewhere. All the complexes must rest on something that is not complex. We have seen that the evidence of observation cannot back this up, because there may be hidden parts that are too small to observe. Unaided reason seems not to dictate the view either. Would it be a contradiction to suppose that the world contained infinite complexity, with ever-smaller parts? There seems no conclusive argument why infinite complexity couldn't be the case. Those who believe that there must be simples have to be basing their belief on some other view, therefore.

There is a philosophical position called atomism, which might be such a basis. An atomist is someone who believes that there are atoms or atomic parts. Here we mean atoms in the original sense of the word: smallest possible things, which are thereby indivisible. The atoms of chemical theory are not atomic in this sense. The atoms of the periodic table contain protons, neutrons, and electrons. An atomist in the philosophical sense believes that everything is built up from smallest possible units, whatever they are. Indeed, you could in theory get a complete description of the world just by stating where all the atoms were and their natures. I say 'just' by doing this but it would be, of course, a mammoth task: bigger than any other completed in human

3. A complex particular

history. But in principle it could be done, which is often all that counts to a philosopher.

It is clear from what is said above that there is no especially strong evidence for any form of atomism. It is more of a philosophical stance than anything else, even though some such atomists believe their view is in a scientific spirit. And although it isn't proven in any conclusive sense, it might nevertheless be a persuasive hypothesis.

This has been by way of prelude to the issue that is really to be addressed in this chapter, which is the relation between wholes and their parts. Is the whole in some sense greater than the sum of the parts, or is it nothing more than the sum? This may seem a strange question to ask, but it is actually of deep philosophical significance, as I hope will become clear.

Now there are many cases where a whole doesn't look to be any more than a sum of parts. Consider a pile of stones, for instance. Maybe there are about a hundred stones in the pile. We can consider the pile as a whole, and in this case it seems to be nothing more than the aggregation of one hundred individual stones. Even in this case, however, we can note that there are some properties of the whole that are not properties of the parts. The pile, let us assume, is one metre high. But none of the individual stones in the pile is a metre high. They are all considerably less than that. Nevertheless, we might think that there is nothing particularly miraculous in this difference. The whole has been formed as a rough pyramid structure. The individual stones are not all that high but they have been arranged in such a way, with some roughly on top of others, that they can combine their individual heights to make an overall height bigger than any one of them. Individual heights, when duly arranged, can make a contribution to the height of the whole. That the whole possesses a property the parts do not is thus perfectly explicable in terms of the parts and their arrangement.

So far: so good. But other cases look a bit more complicated. Think again about the mobile phone. It has some of the same features of the pile of stones. Its length, for instance, is just due to the arrangements of its parts. But some of its properties seem less easy to account for. It has some capacities that are very hard to explain. It is able to transmit and receive sound signals, making it possible to hold a conversation over distance. Most phones now have a broad range of other functions. They can access the Internet, take and store photographs, and play music.

These rather amazing capacities seem of a different kind to the length case. There, the whole had a greater quantity of a property that was already possessed by the parts. They each had lengths that added up. But in the case of some of these operations of the phone, it doesn't seem like there is any individual part that has the capacity in any degree. There is a disanalogy with the length case, therefore. It is not as if the bottom quarter of the phone is able to make a quarter of a call, whereas it presumably has a quarter of the length of the whole. The disanalogy suggests the following: in some cases, a property can come in degrees and a whole just has more of it than the parts; but in other cases, the whole has a property that is not possessed by the parts in any degree. This can be reflected in the way we talk about things. We only call the whole thing a telephone whereas its parts are not telephones. With the pile of stones, however, something I attribute to the whole – its height – is something I can also attribute to the parts in a lesser degree.

The whole truth

There are all sorts of assumptions I have made here, and if you become a professional philosopher you will be trained to spot and criticize them, but as this is not always the most rewarding practice, I will move swiftly on. In particular, I want to draw attention to a distinction that may be interesting.

I have discussed two examples of wholes and how they differed. But perhaps the two examples were very different to begin with. In the first case, we had a mere aggregate of loose parts. I can take a stone off the top of my pile, for instance, and go and add it to another pile. But the mobile phone is more of an integrated whole. If I pull the top half, the bottom half moves with it. It is all properly joined up, which is not to say that it couldn't break apart or that I couldn't prise it open. At that point, it may just become another pile of parts, but until then it seems to have a unity that the pile of stones does not have. For that reason, philosophers sometimes distinguish substances – the integrated wholes – from mere aggregates.

The distinction has some significance. If I replace some of the stones in the pile, I thereby have a different pile because we assume that the identity of an aggregate is determined by what the parts are. If we have different sets of parts, we have different aggregates, even though some parts may at different times be members of different aggregates. But if I replace a part of my mobile phone – the cover, perhaps – it doesn't thereby become a different phone (in the sense of numerical identity, discussed in Chapter 1). Substances can survive a change in their parts in a way that a mere aggregate of parts cannot.

The cases discussed in the remainder of this chapter all concern such substances or integrated wholes because they raise some really challenging questions. The phone had an ability to receive calls, which its parts did not. There is a question to be asked of whether this ability of the whole can be explained entirely in terms of the parts.

When we considered the pile of stones, its whole height and indeed its shape seemed to be just the result of its parts and how they were arranged. But is that also true of the properties of integrated wholes and some of their rather special abilities? Arguably, it still could be. I don't know how a small mobile phone is able to make calls, send emails, and play music. It almost seems as though these abilities are magical. But I also assume it's not really magic. Some technician somewhere knows what the parts are that enable these abilities and how they must be arranged in order for it to function properly. Presumably, workers in factories assembled the parts according to a detailed specification. Whoever understands the technology presumably understands how the parts are able to deliver all the properties and capacities of the whole. In that sense, then, the whole is a sum of parts as long as those parts are correctly arranged.

There are, however, other cases in which this idea has been challenged. Some qualities are thought of as so special that they *emerge* at a certain higher level of reality and nothing like them is to be found at the level of the parts. It is one thing to think of a table as just an assemblage of parts: its four wooden legs arranged at the bottom of a flat wooden surface. But can we think of a human as just various pieces of meat and bone arranged in a certain way? A human is a living thing. Life seems to be a property of the whole organism and something that we don't seem to find among the parts. Another apparent case is consciousness or the mind. We are thinking things also able to experience and reflect on sensations such as pains, itches, and colours. Is the mental something that is entirely explicable in terms of the physical, with brains in particular the focus of attention? Or is the mental a whole new special kind of quality that emerges only at a certain level of nature?

There are two broad positions that philosophers can take on this issue. A *reductionist* is someone who insists that the parts can ultimately explain all the workings of the whole. A reductionist might admit that we do not know all the details yet of how the brain is able to produce consciousness, but they have faith that eventually, when science has discovered all the facts, we will be able to do so. This is a philosophical position. Reductionism has not yet been proved. Those who are tempted by reductionism think, however, that there are already enough cases where the parts have explained the whole that we should generalize and assume it to be the case universally.

In opposition to that view, *emergentism* is the claim that wholes are more than sums of parts. There are various ways in which such an idea can be stated, and different emergentists might not be supporting exactly the same thing. One way of stating the view does so in terms of what we know and what would surprise us or what we would be able to predict. For example, if we knew everything about brains and the way their neurons worked, it can be claimed that even then we would not be able to predict the phenomenon of consciousness, nor what it feels like to experience something. A neuroscientist might know exactly what goes on in the brain when we perceive something red, for instance, but only know what it feels like to see red when they experience it themselves. And if they had never seen something red, they wouldn't know what it was like to see red for all the neuroscientific knowledge they had acquired.

Perhaps what would be *surprising* to us is a mere fact about our psychology, however, and this doesn't quite capture what we think is being claimed in emergentism. In the second way of stating the view, therefore, emergentism is a theory about what there is, not about what surprises us. What the emergentist would really be claiming is that there are genuinely novel phenomena to be found in wholes that are not in their parts, nor their sums, nor in their arrangement. And just as there is a difficulty in knowing whether reductionism is true, and in knowing whether anything is really simple, so there is a difficulty in knowing such emergentism to be true. As things stand, we have no detailed explanation of how the mind emerges from bodily parts, but that could just be because of our ignorance. We have no proven theory yet, and can barely conceive how there could come to be one. Yet we know from the past how science can surprise us with its progress.

Where's the fun in fundamentalism?

There are two pictures that we might have of the world and how all the sciences stand to each other. One is that of an inverted pyramid. At the bottom is one science, upon which everything else is said to rest. For most reductionists, it would be the science of physics at the bottom: perhaps they will say fundamental physics, which deals with particles and the laws governing them. Above that will be the other sciences, such as chemistry, and then higher than that biology. Even higher we will find 'sciences' such as psychology, economics, sociology, and anthropology. The reductionist, however, thinks that all ultimately rest on and are explained by physics. All truths are made true by the arrangements of the fundamental particles and laws of physics.

Opposed to this picture is one in which at least some of the sciences have a degree of independence from each other. Let us consider biology, given that life was an alleged emergent property. Some have attempted to reduce all the truths of biology to truths of biochemistry and say it's all just about DNA, and DNA is reducible to the truths of chemistry and ultimately physics. But there are nevertheless some compelling reasons why we instead have to talk about organisms as wholes rather than sums of parts. The natural selection of evolutionary theory, for instance, selects fairly high-level properties. The long neck gives the giraffe an advantage over its competitors for food rather than anything directly to do with its DNA.

In a way, it seems like the organism as a whole uses its DNA to provide it with what it needs at the level of a whole. If that is true, it would not be that the microscopic physical facts about the giraffe are determining the macroscopic observable properties of the whole: but the other way around. It is whole organisms that live or die, feed or starve, and sometimes reproduce; not their genes or molecules. It seems confused to say that one's genes went for a walk: it is the person who walks. Similarly, it is persons who see things. Even eyes don't see; they are merely what we use to see. And though our body parts can be described as living and organic, they are not organisms, and they would not be capable of life for very long if detached from the whole. Just consider how long a hand would remain alive if detached from the body (yes, I've seen the 1946 film *The Beast with Five Fingers* but that was just fantasy).

These considerations are not conclusive, but they may show that there is at least some attraction in the view we call *holism*. This idea is that wholes in some sense have a priority over the parts.

The notion of priority can be explained in various ways. We saw how reductionists would deny it. They say that the facts about the parts determine the facts about the wholes. The holist has various ways of answering this, as we have seen. One is to invoke cases like evolutionary selection in which facts about wholes seem to be determining facts about the parts. Another way of rejecting reductionism is to deny the title question of this chapter and insist that wholes are indeed more than just sums of parts and their arrangement.

In both philosophy of mind and philosophy of biology, issues of reductionism and emergentism are a central part of the current debate. Metaphysics has a role to play in clarifying what it would be for emergentism to be true. We still haven't made this precise, and it is to be hoped that the metaphysicians of the future will make more progress. What it is for something to be *more than* its parts is an issue we should explore further.

Chapter 4
What is a change?

Our concern so far has been with what there is, but in the most general terms. I know that there are tables, chairs, mobile phones, people, and giraffes, but, to put it in the abstract, we can also say that there are particulars, their properties, and sometimes parts of particulars. One cannot get much more abstract than that. However, one might also be worried that so far our thinking has been led very much by the example of the physical medium-sized object. Certainly, we are surrounded by many things like that but we shouldn't be led into thinking that's all there is. Even if we describe every thing, it is far from clear that we have described everything. Of course, that sounds like just the sort of obscure and paradoxical statement you would get from a philosopher, but it still might be defended. By 'thing', we often mean object, probably physical object. But not everything is a physical object.

We have our particulars, such as cups, cats, and trees, and we have our properties, such as redness, fragility, and four-leggedness. But what of someone blushing, a caterpillar becoming a butterfly, an iron bar heating up, or a book falling from a table? These are events involving changes. And what of longer processes, such as the sun ripening a tomato, the Second World War, or a young baby growing into an old man? What of the history of the entire universe from start to finish? These events and processes certainly seem to be a part of reality. We don't want to deny they exist. They are a real feature of our world. But if we talk just about the particulars and their properties, it seems that we omit them. Listing the particulars and all their properties, unless we make some fancy moves, gives us only a static description of what there is in the world at a time. Change, however, seems as much a part of our world as anything. Without it, nothing would happen. We need to include it in our list of what there is, therefore, and give an account of it.

What's occurring?

Stuff happens. This we know for sure, even if it is all a dream. So what is an event? Is it always a change? And is a process something different? Let us start by considering events.

It should be noted that there are at least two conceptions of events available. One allows that they can be *static*, by which is meant changeless. That the door is brown at midday is on some conceptions regarded as an event. Is that the best way to classify it? Perhaps it is best to call that kind of thing a fact precisely because nothing happens: nothing changes. This may just be a personal preference, however. We can call whatever we want an event as long as we are clear which conception we are using. I will stick with the conception of an event where there is at least some change involved, though, and this is because it is the phenomenon of change that is our main focus in this chapter.

There was mention above of processes, and it is even clearer here that change must be involved, indeed a number of changes. While we might be able to think of an event as involving just a single change, the notion of a process seems to entail multiple changes occurring in a particular sequence. Just as objects can stand in part–whole relations, it seems that exactly the same is true of events. Some events contain other events as parts. Saying 'Good morning' to a neighbour involves the two events of saying 'Good' and saying 'morning' as parts. And for processes, which seem to permit longer and more complex changes, then there are all sorts of parts they can have. The Second World War contained the Battle of Stalingrad as a part, for example, which in turn contained the firing of a bullet from one gun.

Certainly, the notions of event and processes are closely connected, and there may be only a vague divide between them. When does a process become so small that it's just an event; or an event so big that it's a process? We may not be able to impose a very sharp boundary but still maintain that a process suggests a complex series of more than one change in a particular order. The order would be important because if we changed it we would get a different process. The building of a house is a process, for

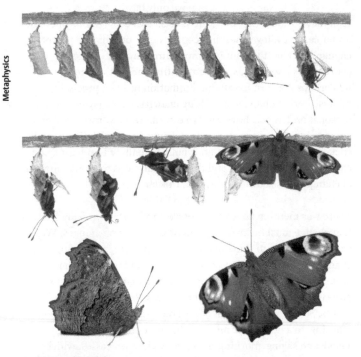

4. Metamorphosis

instance, and if we reverse the order we get something else, like the demolition of a house. We can see, therefore, that the notion of a change looks important for both events and processes, and we should examine this issue more closely.

Who can bear change?

In Chapter 1, there was discussion of particulars and the notion of numerical identity was introduced: the notion of being one and the same thing. This is difficult to state without causing confusion because we want to know when one thing is the very same thing as another. And when they are, then we really have only one thing. For this reason, some have said that identity is not a relation at all: because when it truly holds, then we only have one thing, whereas all genuine relations relate at least two.

Why must something stay the same through a change? Here is the issue. If there is a man with hair in 2010 and a man without hair in 2020, we can say from this information that a change has occurred only if the man with hair in 2010 *is* the man without hair in 2020. If it was one and the same man, then we can say something happened – something changed – a man became bald. There were lots of men with hair in 2010, and there will no doubt be lots of men without hair in 2020, but for a change we need it that a man with hair became a man without hair. It needs to be a single individual who was subject to balding. This idea that change needs a subject is often attributed to Aristotle; indeed, much of metaphysics comes from him.

It seems that we can say the same sort of thing about all small-scale changes, though when we get to larger-scale processes, it may be unclear what the subject of change was. What was the subject of change in the Second World War? The world, perhaps? And some changes involve multiple subjects. Suppose that energy passes from one object to another, perhaps when two snooker balls collide. Is the transfer of energy just one change, involving a relocation of energy, or do we actually have two separate changes here: one the loss of energy by the cue ball and the other the gaining of energy by the object ball? Counting changes is no easy matter and doing so has to be based on a lot of philosophical theory.

Here is such a theory. Changes can come in different varieties. A change could be a gain or loss of a property, the coming into or going out of existence of something, or a change within one property. We can say more about each of these cases.

We are making use of both our notion of particulars and of their properties. Suppose at some point a particular has a property: the tomato is round. But at a later time the tomato no longer has that property. Then a change has occurred. Of course, over that period, the tomato may have gained another property in place of its former roundness: it may have become flat, squashed under the wheel of a passing truck. Again, we can say that a change occurred. Was this just one change or two? Was it a single swapping of one property for another or two related but distinct events: a loss of roundness and a gain of flatness?

The change within a property was another kind of change. The sort of case I am thinking of is where something has a property of length but increases or decreases it. Suppose the cucumber next to the tomato grows in length from 20 centimetres to 30 centimetres. Certainly, a change has occurred, and no doubt it was a gradual one in so far as to get from 20 to 30 centimetres the cucumber's length passes through all the intermediate lengths in between, rather than jumping straight from one to the other. The change looks like a process in this respect. But the point of it is that length is a single property that can come in degrees, magnitudes, or varying quantities. Another way of thinking of it is to say that there are various determinate lengths that fall under the determinable notion of length. When the cucumber grows, it keeps the same determinable property of length but changes its determinate lengths, one switching for another.

There was one other kind of change that I suggested: something coming into or going out of existence. Here, the change does not occur in the properties of something but to the thing itself. It comes into existence or ceases to be. These are very puzzling notions. A new car can roll off the production line, for example, newly created, and some years later, it can go to a scrap yard to be broken up. Perhaps nothing really is created or destroyed but, rather, parts – and parts of parts – are merely assembled in different combinations or disassembled and used elsewhere. Remember being told that energy could neither be created nor destroyed? It makes you wonder where it came from in the first place. But we need not ponder that for too long because all we need in order to say that a change has occurred is a coming into or going out of existence in the relatively weak sense of parts having made a new whole or having being disassembled from a whole. I know that a change has occurred when my car is taken apart even if those parts, or some parts of the parts, remain in existence.

There is a challenge to such theories of change, however. The Aristotelian notion of there being a subject of change, which endures through the change, has been questioned in more modern times. Perhaps this is because we have come to think of space and time as more alike than we used to. This needs explanation.

A human body has spatial parts. It has a top half and a bottom half. There is an arm, a heart, a toe, and much more besides. These could all be thought of as being spatial parts of the body: parts in space. But then why not also allow that there are temporal parts too: parts in time? There is the part of that body that existed in 2010 and another that existed in 1970. There is a part that existed for just one minute at 12.05 today. Certainly, if there is a close analogy between space and time, it suggests there should be temporal parts.

But why is this significant? Some have thought that temporal parts would be a good way to explain change. The problem such philosophers identify is that in the old Aristotelian theory, in which things endure through change, different qualities have to be ascribed to one and the same particular. The tomato has both the property of being green and the property of being red. The cucumber is both 20 centimetres long and 30 centimetres long. If one believes that things have temporal parts, however, one can say that it is different things that have these incompatible properties. It was one temporal part of the tomato that was green and a different temporal part that was red. The analogy with space again holds. We are not alarmed to hear that a tomato is both red and green if it is one spatial part that is red and another that is green. If there are different parts, either spatial or temporal, that bear the incompatible properties, then any apparent contradiction is dissolved.

The wholly presence

If you don't accept temporal parts, you have to find some other explanation of how something seems able to bear incompatible properties. In the Aristotelian theory, a particular is said to be wholly present at every time in which it exists. It is not a temporal part of the tomato that is red but the whole tomato. Indeed, we say things like 'the tomato is red'. We don't say 'the tomato's temporal-part is red'. Then again, perhaps language use is no reliable guide to metaphysics.

The Aristotelian view is known as *endurantism* because wholly present particulars endure through changes. But how can the view explain the bearing of incompatible properties? The answer, of course, is that those incompatible properties are borne at different times. The tomato was green last week while it is red this week. This reply comes at a cost, however. It means that properties are not held pure and simple by particulars. They would always have to be held relative to something else, namely a particular time, and this complicates our account of what it is to have a property. In contrast, those who believe in temporal parts, who are known as *perdurantists*, can say that the temporal part has the property pure and simple, with no need for any further relational element to be involved.

When something changes, we should not see it as a single thing bearing contrary properties, according to perdurantism, but as different things – temporal parts – bearing those properties. If the view is an attempt to explain change, then it means that each of those temporal parts must themselves be changeless. Were a temporal part to be capable of undergoing any change itself, then the problem that originally motivated the view would resurface. So it is clear that there must be a different temporal part for every slight change.

Such change would also have to be reconceptualized radically. Instead of the idea of a subject of change enduring through change of properties, what we would have would be a succession of things with static properties, only very slightly different from the things that immediately precede and follow them. Change would to an extent be an illusion created by the succession of such temporal parts. But this idea is not alien to us. It is rather like that of old-fashioned film used at a cinema. Each individual frame of the film strip is a changeless, unmoving picture. But they are arranged in a sequence on a device that is able to turn over the pictures very quickly. And when viewed in rapid succession, it looks like movement. For perdurantism, our world operates very much like this.

There are nevertheless some good reasons why we might be suspicious of this theory. For a start, it looks more like a denial of change than a theory of it. Each of the temporal parts is entirely changeless, and thus all the kinds of change described above reduce to the coming into and going out of existence (of temporal parts). Perhaps more seriously, the notion of a thing as a succession of temporal parts is problematic and thereby so is the account of change that follows from it.

In what sense do a number of changeless temporal parts all belong to the same thing? If one follows the letter of the theory, they don't. There are no enduring things, as we have seen. Rather, what we take to be a thing is just some construction out of the sequence of static parts. Therefore, a collection of parts needs to be connected up in an appropriate way so that they make what we take to be an enduring thing. This would be a matter of finding the right relations to hold between the parts. Succession in time would be one requirement, for presumably two distinct temporal parts that existed at the same time couldn't be a part of the same thing. Perhaps causation is another relation, where the earlier temporal parts cause the later ones to be (causation is the topic of our next chapter).

It appears that we need to have these particulars constructed from the succession of parts in some such way before we can speak of changes having occurred. In other words, to say that a man has grown bald we need first to construct the man out of the temporal parts by relating them together in some way. Our problem was that we can only say a change has occurred if the hairy man in 2010 is the bald man in 2020. But this would rely crucially on showing that the hairy man is properly related to the bald man.

We have the problem in perdurantism, therefore, of suitably connecting all these distinct parts. But do we really want our changes to be constituted by ultimately changeless components? Is it really plausible that the seemingly smooth changes we see around us are just successions of static parts? It would be a jerky world, jumping from one state to another, though supposedly so quickly that we don't notice the joins. Here, the appeal of endurantism may return into the reckoning but in a modified form. We might see the world as changing continuously. A continuous, extended change would be a process. Perhaps dynamic processes compose the world, then, rather than it being constructed from a succession of changeless parts. The idea would be that processes in our world occur in smooth, indivisible, and integrated wholes.

When you consider the dissolution of sugar in tea, for instance, this seems like a natural and continuous process. Perdurantism would depict this as some collection of disconnected temporal parts that just happen to fall in the right sort of relations so that we stick them together. But maybe all the parts of this process are essential to it. To be soluble is to be disposed towards this process, and it is essential that the process be precisely this. We may say the same of lots of other processes: they seem to come in integrated, continuous wholes. Consider photosynthesis, the human life cycle, or crystallization. Do we really want to see these as collections of parts that become joined together willy-nilly and which could in principle have occurred in any old order? I would suggest not, for processes seem to offer a plausible case of the whole being greater than the sum of the parts.

It is time to move on from change to something that is clearly connected. We are already starting to encroach on the subject matter of our next chapter, which will be one of the greatest of all philosophical problems: causation.

Chapter 5
What is a cause?

I kick a football towards the goal and it goes in. My team-mates come to congratulate me. Why? Because I scored the goal. It was my doing. I caused the goal. Later, I knock over a cup and it smashes. I get the blame. Why? Again, responsibility falls on me for something I caused to happen. Humans need not be involved in such examples. A hurricane causes tree damage and flooding; or corroded rivets cause a bridge to fail.

Sometimes one thing is connected to another and this is very significant. My kicking of the ball was connected to it moving. But if we considered the totality of events in the world, most of them would have no direct connection. Napoleon's defeat at Waterloo, I assume, has no connection to you scratching your nose just when you did. There might be some very indirect connection, via many other intervening events, but it would be such a tenuous connection that it wouldn't be significant. There are other cases where it is in dispute whether one sort of thing is connected to another. Tobacco companies denied for years that there was any connection between smoking and cancer, for example. Mystics claim they can communicate thoughts directly to others or move objects by their will alone, while others deny that both telepathy and telekinesis are real. Effectively, this is a denial of a causal connection.

We have been considering the general kinds of thing that make up our world. We have looked at properties, particulars, complex particulars, and then changes. Causes look to be another important category that we need to consider. This topic is closely related to that of a change, though it is not exactly the same. Many, perhaps most, of the changes in the world are caused, but not all of them need be. On some accounts, the universe originated with a Big Bang, which was a huge coming into existence. That sounds like a change, therefore, but we are also told that it is uncaused because nothing existed before that might have caused it. We can distinguish, therefore, between changes that were caused and those that were uncaused. So a change and a cause are different things. Indeed, even when they go together, we should say that they are different things. The cause would be what produced the change, where it is indeed a caused change. And just to separate the two notions even more sharply, we can also say that there are causes without changes. Sometimes causes produce stability or equilibrium. Magnets may hold together, for instance, with nothing occurring. But this seems as clear a cause as any other example.

Causes everywhere

The understanding of causation is one of the biggest of all philosophical tasks: and not just because philosophers have been worrying about it for centuries. It is vital we have an account of causation because it holds almost everything together, hence Hume's description of it as 'the cement of the universe'. We find it virtually everywhere, and without it nothing would matter to anything else. Archduke Franz Ferdinand getting shot is significant, for instance, only because it caused his death and, so it's said, caused the First World War. Indeed, Gavrilo Princip pulled the trigger only because he believed it might cause a bullet to exit the gun and the bullet might then cause Franz Ferdinand's death.

Any action we perform seems premised on the idea that it will cause stuff to happen. I hammer a nail, for instance, only because I expect it to cause the nail to sink into the wall. If hammering had no connection with an outcome, it would be a totally pointless activity. Suppose it didn't cause the nail to sink into the wall. Or suppose when you hammered, some random change occurred: the nail could evaporate, or vanish, or turn into a chicken. If there were no causal connections between anything, our world would be entirely unpredictable to any degree. Our predictions are not entirely reliable as things stand but reliable enough for us to get by. The fact that they are is down to there being causal connections. Establishing what they are is often of vital importance to us. Identifying the cause of a disease could be crucial, for instance. We can save lives by keeping people away from the causes of death. Alternately, we also want to find medicines that cause people to get better even if they've contracted the disease.

These examples convey the importance of causation. This gives philosophers something of a duty to understand and tell us what causal connections are. But here it gets difficult.

Fighting the cause

One problem is a traditional thought that comes from David Hume, whose ideas on causation continue to shape the philosophical debate (*A Treatise of Human Nature*, Book I, 1739). Hume told us that causal connections were unobservable. We can see one event, such as someone taking a pill, and a second event when they get better, but we never see the causal connection between the two events. How then do we know that the drug caused the recovery? The problem is deeper than merely that I cannot see inside someone's body (very easily). Even in the simplest case, Hume alleges that we can never see the causal connection. You can see the kick and you can see the ball move,

5. David Hume

but you cannot see any causation between the kick and the ball moving.

If none of us can see causal connections, why then do we believe that they are real? Hume had a view on this. The main reason why we think that the first event caused the second is that it is part of a pattern. Whenever I have seen someone kick a ball, it has been followed by the ball moving. I am just seeing one event followed by another in each instance; but I also know that whenever I have seen an event of the first kind, it has been followed by an event of the second kind.

For many followers of Hume, this is more than just a point about our knowledge of causes. It is also a popular view to say that this is an account of causation in reality. Until you have read philosophy, you might think that one event can make another happen. There is some kind of push or compulsion between the first event and the second. Humeans, however, as well as saying that we have no knowledge of any such push, say that we need no such thing to understand the world. There need be nothing more than the events and the patterns into which they fall. Lots of kicking-of-ball-type events have occurred and lots of footballs have moved. It just so happens that the kicking events were followed by the balls moving. The world is then being understood as a patchwork of unconnected events, some of which just happen to fall into patterns.

Consider, for instance, if you had a big bucket of mosaic tiles. You could give them a shake and then pour them out on to the floor. They would effectively have fallen in a random arrangement. But even here, as I study the tiles hard, I might be able to see patterns. I might see that a red tile is always next to a blue tile, or that a square tile is always next to a triangular one. As I think harder and harder, I might notice even more elaborate patterns: a circular yellow tile is always next to either a green square or an orange triangle, and so on. We might then say that this is all we are doing when we investigate the world scientifically. If taking the medicine is always followed by recovery from the disease, then what more can we want of causation?

There is another thought, however, that has tempted some towards a different kind of view. The view is also in Hume, who proposed two different types of theory. One was that causation consisted just in regularity. The other theory requires a different explanation. We often come to understand what causes what through experimenting in the world. As a child, you might pull and release the string on the back of your dolly's neck and find that the doll talks. You can do this a few times and see that pulling the string is regularly followed by the doll talking. Arguably, however, to really get causal knowledge, you need also to know that the doll will not speak unless you pull the string.

6. Causation

After all, if the doll talks all the time, whether you pull its string or not, you would be unlikely to think pulling the string caused the talking. An insight follows from this. We might think of a cause as one event followed by another where if the first had not occurred, the second would not have either. These are almost Hume's exact words.

But how do I know that? I can see that one event is followed by another, but how do I know that if the first had not occurred, when as a matter of fact it did, the second event would not have occurred? There is a worry that one's belief that the second event would not have occurred would actually be informed by the belief that the first caused the second. This is not good because the theory is supposed to be telling us what it is for an event to cause something, so it cannot depend on a prior notion of cause (for then it would be a circular explanation).

There are two answers to this question. One employs some elaborate metaphysics, while the other is a bit more down to earth.

49

The philosophers' answer is that while in our world both the first and second events occur, there's another world that is just like ours except that, there, the first event doesn't occur. If, in that world, the second event doesn't occur either, then it's the case in our world that the first event caused the second. In other words, given that both events did occur in our world, we can only consider the possibility of the first not occurring in some other possible world. And the world to consider is the one most like ours but for the fact that the first event did not occur. This would flesh out what Hume's second theory wanted of causation. Event A causes B because in the world just like ours except for the fact that A did not occur, B did not occur either.

This talk of other possible worlds may seem like a metaphysical extravagance. We shall encounter such worlds again in Chapter 8. But there is arguably another way of knowing that if one event had not occurred, a second would not. This is a more scientific kind of approach that is regularly put into practice. We could perform an actual experiment instead of thinking of what goes on in other worlds. To do so, we would need to set up two test cases that were as similar as possible in every respect we could think of. Then, in one test case, we introduce the event in question. In the second case, we don't. Then we see whether the introduced factor made a difference to the outcomes or not. John Stuart Mill called this the method of difference.

According to some, this method is the way that in reality we discover causes. To see whether a medicine works, for example – and by works, I mean whether it causes recovery – we divide a large sample of people at random into two groups. If the numbers are big enough and the randomization genuine, then we should get two groups that are sufficiently similar. We then give the trial medicine to one group and none to the second group. The second group get a placebo, just in case merely believing you're being treated can itself cause recovery. If the first group gets better and the second doesn't, it is declared that the medicine caused the recovery. This kind of experiment is called a randomized controlled trial and is purported to demonstrate for large numbers what Hume and Mill had suggested in theory. We are in a position to see in an actual experiment that without the first thing (the taking of medicine), we would not have the second (recovery).

Here is a big concern with these kinds of theory, which are known as counterfactual dependence theories of causation. Can this difference be really what causation is all about? Perhaps it allows us to understand what causes what, but it doesn't actually tell us what it is for one thing to cause another. Look at it this way. The group who took the medicine would have got better whether or not there was another group elsewhere who took a placebo. Suppose that because of an administrative error, the group due to take the placebo were forgotten and that part of the trial never occurred. Would that have meant the first group, although they got better, weren't caused to do so by the medicine? If they took it and recovered, they may well question whether anything happening elsewhere was of any relevance at all to the question of how well the medicine worked on them. Similarly, if I kick a football and it moves, how could the question of whether my kick caused it to move be affected by what has happened in some other possible world or some duplicate test situation in which no one kicked a ball?

The thought behind this line of reasoning is that when we have two events, A and B, the question of whether A caused B is about A and B alone and any connection there is or isn't between them. What is happening at other times and places seems like it ought to be irrelevant. Such a view is known as *singularism*. How can one justify such a view? One way would be to say that what counts is, for example, whether the medicine has a genuine power to produce recovery. In particular, I might want to know whether this very pill has a power to make this particular patient better. If it does, then when taken in the correct way, it causes the recovery. Similarly, when you kick the football, what makes it move is that causal power of the kick. Only the foot and the ball are relevant to this.

This leaves us something to say about the two Humean views that we considered. The first was that causation consisted in regularity. The singularist will allege that there is something problematic in this view. It seems to mix up particular causal claims and general ones. A particular claim would be that this drug made this patient better. A general causal claim would be that this type of drug could make anyone better. When we allege that smoking causes cancer, we are making a general causal claim. The theory was that for one particular event to cause another was for it to be part of a pattern: in other words, there had to be a general causal truth of which the particular case was just one instance.

Hume's opponent may insist that the order of explanation is the wrong way round here. The reason there are general causal truths is because there are particular ones that we generalize about. This particular man smoked and it caused him to get cancer, and that man was also caused to get cancer by smoking, and so on, and we can generalize all such particular causal claims to say that smoking in general causes cancer.

For Hume the bell tolls

The connection between particular and general causal truths may not be quite so clear and simple, however. We all know there are some who manage to smoke all their lives without getting cancer. Nevertheless, we still think that there is a truth that smoking causes it. So what does the general causal truth mean or entail? We could say the following. Smoking tends to produce cancer. In many cases, it indeed does, but it might not do so in every case. The power is there – tobacco is carcinogenic – but there are cases where it fails to do its evil work. Someone may just have the right kind of genes that are able to prevent tobacco's effects. There can be a general causal truth, therefore, that doesn't apply to all the individual cases. Thus, a randomized controlled trial could show that a drug is effective against a certain disease, but this may be based only on statistics. Some people in the trial group might get better but not all. In that case, it is quite conceivable that the drug has no effect on me individually.

There may be very good reasons why a cause works on some things of a certain kind but not all. Hume knew of the causal powers view as an alternative to his own. But he thought that such a view would mean that causes had to necessitate their effects. If there is a power for a certain effect, he argued, it would mean that it *had* to produce its effect when it operated. But this need not be the position. A power might only dispose towards a certain effect. There can be cases where it succeeds in producing that effect, but in other cases it could be prevented from doing its job. The effects that we see around us are often the result of many different factors working together. When a paper aeroplane is thrown, for instance, its trajectory is determined by its aerodynamic shape but also gravity, gusts of wind, electrostatic attractions and repulsions, and so on. It could be that some of those factors dispose it in one direction while others dispose it in an opposite one.

In the case of the medicine, then, we might find that the drug has a power to cure and succeeds in doing so in many cases. But one particular individual might find it has no effect. Perhaps they are constitutionally immune to it, or they have a lifestyle that cancels it out, or they have a diet that aggravates the disease, or whatever the case may be. Presence of the medicine, even though it frequently produces recovery, needn't always do so. Understood this way, powers do not necessitate their effects. Hume thought it was a reason to reject a powers view that they could be prevented or interfered with. What we've seen is that they don't work through necessitating, but this is no reason to reject powers, properly understood.

The familiar name of Aristotle appears again. He seemed to think causal powers were a part of reality. Hume's dissent came much later but had just as strong an impact on philosophy, and there is still a big divide among contemporary metaphysicians between Humeans and non-Humeans. The key dispute seems to be between those who think the cause really does produce its effect and those who think there is nothing more than a pattern of events, with no real connection between them. As a word of warning, however, it should be noted that Humeans contend that by 'produce', 'cause', 'power', and so on, we can mean nothing more than regular succession, or that if the cause had not been there, neither would the effect. Everything a realist says about causation, one can translate into Humean terms about the pattern of events. It then becomes hard to even articulate the difference between Humeans and their opponents.

Chapter 6
How does time pass?

We have been considering what there is in terms of some of the most general categories. There are particulars and properties, but there are also things like wholes, parts, changes, and causes. The latter two could not exist unless there was also something else: time. For a change to occur, there must at least be something at one time that is no longer at a later time, or vice versa. Philosophers argue about whether there could be time without change, but it surely looks certain that there could not be change without time.

What is this thing we call time? This is perhaps a question we have all thought about, and in doing so we will have been engaging in metaphysics. One thought is that time is some thing itself and acts as a background in which events are situated. We think of this time as flowing and having a direction. It can pass you by. You need to keep up with it and not waste it. It has reached a certain point. Perhaps it's a finite resource. This image of time may resemble the flow of a river. It moves at a certain pace, passing certain points along the river bank. At your birth, you jump on a raft and the river takes you downstream, passing all the signposted years on the bank along the way. At your death, you jump off the raft, and the flow of time carries on along its way without you.

7. The direction of time

Some of these thoughts do seem puzzling, however. We speak of time flowing but, while we can measure the speed of a river, can we really do anything similar for time? If time passes, how quickly does it pass? Presumably one second per second? Does that make sense? Could there be any other answer? If I get a paddle on my raft, could I go faster or even slower than time itself? And we say that time has a direction. We say it goes forwards rather than backwards, but what are we asserting with this? Perhaps time is after all going backwards. What would it look like if it did?

Treating time as a thing in itself, having some kind of existence independently of the events situated within it, also suggests that there could be a period of time in which nothing happens. Is this really a possibility? How do I know that there hasn't just been a gap of a year in which everything stood still and then resumed again? Or perhaps it was a gap of two years.

When we discuss time, we find it so hard to grasp that we have to resort to metaphors. These may be misleading, however. I might say that time has passed me by, or that a long time has passed, but these can't literally be true. Length is something attributable to space and passing is attributable to motion, as in a dog running past me. Maybe the thought is that a certain event or process – your teenage years, for example – come from the future, into the present, but are then gone into your past. You can wave them goodbye, just as when you see the dog running up, for a time he is by your side, but then he is gone again. Does time pass like this?

How soon is now?

There are two models of time that have been debated by metaphysicians over the past century. I will spend some time on the first.

Think of an event such as the assassination of President Abraham Lincoln. For those living before 1865, the event was in the future. For us, the event is in the past. And on 14 April 1865 at about 10.15pm Washington DC time, it was a present event. Should we understand this case in terms of the spatial analogy? Did the event creep up on people, briefly attain presentness, and then go off into the past? Or is there some other way we should understand it?

There is a view that still has some respectability in which events have temporal properties of a sort. The assassination of Lincoln has a property of being past. A number of events have the property of being present, such as the event of you reading this sentence (and think of all the other events going on while you are reading). Many events have a property of being future, a property that might be called futurity. The Qatar football World Cup, the next UK general election, the solar eclipse of 21 September 2025, and the Earth's human population reaching eight billion are all examples, as far as can be told in 2012.

And here is where we might get some sense of the direction of time. Events always are first future, then present, then past. It never goes in the opposite direction, as far as we know. If backwards time travel is possible, that might complicate it, but it seems the three temporal properties are always possessed in that order. I am, of course, treating events as particulars here rather than what metaphysicians call types. The Olympics occurs every four years, but by that we mean a type of event. Each particular Games is a one-off, and it is such events-as-particulars to which I am referring. These events 'flow' from the future, through the present, and into the past.

Temporal properties would have some strange features. It seems they would be able to come and go in different combinations. What was future may now be past. The 2025 eclipse is in the future as I write this, but eventually it will be in the past. Perhaps you are reading this after it occurred. This shows me from my 2012 position that it has a property of being *future past*; that is, a future event will eventually become past (by October 2025, for instance). And there is also a past future. Lincoln's assassination was the future in 1860 but it isn't any longer. His assassination hasn't been future since 1865. It might then be wondered how things can have qualities such as these and what is happening when they undergo a change in respect of them. Is it that there are lots of things standing around somewhere with the property of futurity, waiting until they attain the property of presentness? Are there future people who are longing to be present, thinking to themselves 'How soon is now?'? And where do they go when they attain a property of pastness? Does anything really have that property, or is it merely that they go out of existence?

No time like the present

There is a view that only the present is real; appropriately, it's called *presentism*. This could be thought of as a response to some of the questions just posed. For isn't it absurd to say there are things with the properties of futurity and pastness? To exist seems a condition of bearing properties, but one could argue that future and past things have no existence at all. Barack Obama was born in 1961. Wouldn't it be misleading to suggest that he existed in 1959 though at that time with the property of futurity? And Julius Caesar did exist for a time but he doesn't now. It would again be wrong-headed to say that he exists now but with the property of pastness. It seems an option, therefore, to say that instead of there being three temporal properties, we should instead substitute a simple notion of existence and allow that things come into and go out of existence. When present, they are real. After that, they are not.

That seems a sensible view, but here are some issues to be considered. First, how long does the present last? Is it today, or this minute, or just a second? At 20:50 in the evening, midday today is surely past. Indeed, even 20:49 is past, and two seconds ago also. The present seems like a tiny sliver. We can wait for its existence, but it is too quickly gone. Indeed, if there is a smallest unit of time – some micro-micro-second, which we might call an *instant* – then the present seems only to be as long as that instant. If we deny that, and argue instead that the present has some extension, then how long should we allow it to be? Two minutes? That looks an arbitrary figure. And yet if we don't allow the present to have some temporal extension, it seems almost to vanish to nothingness.

Here is a second problem for presentism. The notion of the present is challenged by relativity theory. I may think that the sun is now shining, and it thus seems to be part of the present. But I'm also told that it takes 8 minutes and 19 seconds for the light of the Sun to reach Earth. Absolute simultaneity has been challenged in physics, and we are told it's illegitimate to speak of two spatially separated events being simultaneous. You could view two stars collapsing in distant galaxies and it might look as if they are collapsing at the same time. But if one is much closer to your telescope than the other, then those events are not really simultaneous at all. There is a problem then of what exactly we mean by the present when it seems always relative to a position or a viewpoint. We could settle for a purely subjective account of the present – it's what appears to be *now*, for some viewer – but many of us don't want our metaphysics to be so dependent on one's point of view. We like to feel that we are dealing in objective, eternal, and immutable truths, unaffected by our human perspective on things.

Speaking of which, there is a further problem for presentism. Although Caesar is not alive, there is a strong sense in which he is nevertheless real, even now. There are facts about him – he crossed the Rubicon – and there must be something in virtue of which those facts are true. If only the present exists, what makes it true that there was a Second World War or an assassination of Lincoln? Wouldn't it be wise to say that those past occurrences and things are a part of our reality even if they are not present? Given the above considerations from relativity theory, there are even some past facts that I can still see: for example, what the Sun looked like eight minutes ago. What is there to stop someone rewriting history if we deny any reality to what happened in the past?

Getting pasturized

There is a view, therefore, that treats the past and future differently. It's one thing to call absurd the idea of future people standing around waiting to be born. But the past is not quite the same. It did exist. It was present. And in this sense, it should be counted part of the totality of reality. Being a part of reality but not in the present could account for our property of pastness, then.

This view is often likened to a growing block. One could think of the present as a thin layer on top of a big solid cuboid. New layers keep being added to it all the time on its top surface. Caesar, and all that he did, is there in the block, some little way down. When we speak of what exists, there are two things we could mean. What exists now is only the top surface of our block, which is in that position only fleetingly. Perhaps it is just a few molecules of the block thick. But we could also mean by what exists the entire block, which is the whole of existence from its start until present. The past is now part of this. But as new layers are added on to the growing block, former present events recede into the distance. We could say they become pasturized, just in virtue of having a new future built upon them.

We have moved, therefore, from a view that privileges the present to one that privileges both the present and the past, though not the future. This second view still has to face the problem of what counts as present: of how thin it is and of the problem of absolute simultaneity. To an extent, the problem remains of treating presentness and pastness as properties of events or things. The growing block picture has merely dispensed with the property of futurity.

I said earlier that there were two models of time philosophers had debated. The first tries to explain the passage of time in terms of events and things having a property of presentness, pastness, or possibly futurity. But we have seen that this leads us into saying strange things at every turn. Perhaps the problem is that we started by looking for a theory that would satisfy an image we had in which time flowed: it passed like the water in a river. There is a different way of understanding the temporal sequence, however. In this view, there is no property of presentness, nor pastness, nor futurity. Instead, we can only say that the events and things in our world stand in relations of order to each other. They are temporally related and to that extent can stand in a sequence.

Early, late, or on time

The basic relations out of which such a sequence could be built are being *earlier than*, being *later than*, and being *simultaneous with*.

Obama's birth is certainly earlier than his death, but it was later than the assassination of Lincoln, which itself was earlier than the assassination of Kennedy. The notion of simultaneity has been challenged, as we have seen, though that applies only to events at different places. I might thus legitimately still say something like Obama's birth was simultaneous with his first breath, given that those events occurred at the same place.

The flow or passage of time could be seen, on this view, as a misleading metaphor created to accommodate the *earlier than* and *later than* relations that hold between things and events. There is no change of properties, from presentness to pastness. The temporal relations between events in this new series hold for all times. It is at any time the case that Obama's birth is later than Lincoln's death. Nothing has to pass from one state to another. Nor do we need to see time as thing-like, such as a medium within which events occur. So perhaps there need be no worry about whether there could be time without change. Instead, we could just think of all the world's events being placed in an order – what was before what – and then we have the sequence of time.

This last idea gets us to the heart of a very important matter: one on which there is another Platonist–Aristotelian divide. The divide has lurked in the background throughout this chapter. Do we treat time as an objectively real thing, existing in its own right, whether or not any events are happening within it? Or do we think that time is nothing more than the ordered sequence of events?

At the start of the chapter, I almost suggested that we needed the reality of time as a background against which changes could occur. But an Aristotelian way of looking at it would be to start with change – maybe all of the world's changes – and see time as some sort of construction from them. If the thought of everything standing still for a year – and then resuming unnoticeably where it left off – seems absurd, then the Aristotelian view is probably more appealing. Time would be judged to have started with the first event: the Big Bang, if you like. The idea of there being anything 'before the Big Bang' would be absurd for an Aristotelian but not necessarily for a Platonist. The latter might also countenance a serious answer to the question of at what time the Big Bang occurred, as if there were some kind of godly astronomical clock that dated everything. For an Aristotelian, the first event was the point at which the clock started ticking.

One may have some attraction towards coupling this Aristotelian view with what is called *eternalism* about events and things. We considered privileging the present, or the present and past, but the eternalist takes all events as equally real even if from one perspective they are future. I don't know whether the 2020 Olympic Games will pass off successfully or not, but, if they do, an eternalist takes them just to be as much a part of reality as anything. This may sound confusing. Trading on the image of the block again, the eternalist takes reality to be one huge block of everything that ever was and will be. We are located some place in the middle, able to look back at what occurred earlier than us but unable to see what is later than our perspective. But it's all just as real.

When we consider what exists, we are sometimes tempted to think of the question only three-dimensionally: of what exists in the whole of space. But shouldn't we be thinking four-dimensionally instead: about what exists in the whole of space and time? Obama's birth is earlier than his death. We cannot maintain this if one of those events is not yet real (as I write this in 2012). Why do I say this? The thought is that a relation is real only if its relata – the things it relates – are real. Obama's birth could not bear a relation to something non-existent. We must grant reality to Obama's death, therefore, while of course hoping there will be some time to go before it.

This may sound like a tempting account as it does away with the idea of time as a flowing medium. But there could also be a worry

How does time pass? (side text)

that it ignores something fundamental about time. It certainly does seem like there is a present that has a special quality about it. We may allow all times to be equally real in so far as they are all existent, but couldn't one also argue that the present has something that neither the past nor future has? What is that? Well, it's what's happening *now* – at one place and point of view at the very least. And does the view of time as nothing more than a relative ordering of events have the resources to explain what any kind of *now* is?

A further issue in the philosophy of time is worthy of mention. There is the question of its topography. We sometimes think of time as a single straight line. It has a beginning, it runs its course, and has an end. But there are other ways of picturing it. Perhaps the line continues indefinitely. Time might not be a finite resource. And it might continue infinitely in both directions. On the other hand, it could branch out as it progresses. There might be two separate timelines branching out from a single source, based on some significant difference. A more radical idea would be that time goes round in a circle. What caused the first event in the history of the universe? Perhaps it was the last moment in the history of the universe. These debates remain live, and perhaps the reader can see how our stances on some of the issues discussed earlier might inform our decisions on these latest options.

Chapter 7
What is a person?

Some of the examples of particulars in Chapter 1 were
things like tables and chairs. They are lifeless and inanimate.
Some particulars, on the other hand, are animals, such as
cats and dogs. But people are also particulars, and it is arguable
that there is something special about them. People matter
so much to us. Are there metaphysical grounds for their special
status? They have minds and, some think, souls or spirits.
What then counts for a person to persist through time could be
different from what it is for a purely physical object such as
a table to persist.

By a person, I don't necessarily mean a human being. All
persons that I know probably are human beings, but there seems
at least the conceptual possibility of a non-human person.
The philosopher John Locke saw this (*Essay Concerning Human
Understanding*, 1690), noting that any properly intelligent
animal could in principle qualify as a person. And, on the other
hand, a human being might in principle not qualify as a
person. The latter would be controversial because removing
the status of person from a human seems one of the worst
things we could do to them. Nevertheless, it has been
wondered whether humans in persistent vegetative states still
count as persons.

What would qualify something as a person, then? Locke mentions intelligence and, more generally, we might think that a person is a thinking thing, capable of consciousness: an experiencer of thoughts and sensations. They might have memory, beliefs, hopes, and emotions. Persons are also able to perform actions, and this makes them moral agents, responsible for what they do. If an animal was capable of any of these things, or even if a computer was, then we might think them worthy of the status of a person.

Thanks for the memories

Because this seems to be what makes something a person, there is a very important implication, which Locke saw. While we think that a table persists through time in virtue of having the same physical parts, we do not think this true of persons. There are some difficult issues here. As we saw in Chapter 4, a substance can indeed survive a change in some of its parts. When you replace the spark plugs in your car engine, it remains the same car. And in the case of organisms, we know that the body is constantly renewing itself: shedding old dead skin and replacing it with new matter. But in these cases, it is still physical features that we use to identify a thing and re-identify it over time. Locke thought that in the case of persons, it was memory, or psychological continuity, that was key to a person's survival. Given that my body has probably renewed itself a number of times since I was a naughty schoolchild, what it is that makes me the same person as that naughty schoolchild is that I remember being him.

We have no need to restrict our psychology to memory, however. After all, I've forgotten most of the things I've done. But I share some of the same beliefs as that schoolchild, some of the same hopes and some of the same psychological foibles and insecurities. Not everything is the same. That child thought Father

Christmas existed, whereas I don't. But such changes between him and me happened gradually, a bit at a time, which means there was some continuity through the changes. It seems we have to allow this kind of flexibility into the account.

The following is a possibility. I don't remember being the small child who ran home from school one day (though my mother has told me the story often enough). But I do remember being the person who graduated with honours from Huddersfield Polytechnic, so on Locke's account, I am identical with him. But the problem is, I'm supposing, that the young man who graduated did at that time remember being the child who ran home from school. So the young graduate is identical with the small child, whereas I, because I don't remember running home from school, am not. Yet I'm identical with the graduate. Memory fades over time, so we need to allow gradual change and continuity. Wittgenstein gave us a nice image to think of here. The individual strands that constitute a rope go only so far through it. There is no single strand that goes from one end to the other. But through a series of overlapping parts, the rope manages to stretch from one end to another. Our psychological continuity must be like this.

The idea that it is our minds that make us what we are has tempted some to an even stronger claim. Descartes thought that there were two parts to us: our bodies and our minds (*Meditations on First Philosophy*, 1641). And it was the mind that was really vital to us. We are essentially thinking things. For a time, we are embodied in a mortal organism but, thought Descartes, it was possible for us to survive the deaths of our bodies. Our minds could live on after death, as immortal souls. This is a strongly metaphysical claim, yet perhaps a common one, certainly among those who are religious. Along with a belief in the existence of God, perhaps it is one of the most common of all metaphysical beliefs, which shows that more of us are metaphysicians than we think.

Philosophers are always liable to spoil a good party, however. They cast their sceptical and quizzical gaze upon many a comforting belief. There are at least two worries they try to give to those who believe in souls. The first is what would count as a spiritual substance. The second is how such a spiritual substance could interact with a physical one, as is supposed to happen when mind and body are united during the regular period of one's life.

Descartes thought that the essence of matter – he used the term *body* – was extension. The idea is that material things – physical portions of matter – are extended in space. They have dimensions: height, length, and breadth. One could also add that they have a location in space too, though perhaps this is only relative to other objects. Extension isn't enough, however. Descartes seems to be wrong here because a volume of empty space could have an extension. There is an empty area in the middle of my room, for instance, that is a metre cubed. It is extended but it's not a physical thing. What we need is that the extended area of space is occupied. But occupied by what? A physical thing? That would be to go in a circle. We are trying to say what a physical thing is. A notion of *impenetrability* has been suggested, or *solidity*. The essence of matter is to be extended and impenetrable. Presumably, we have to complicate the story a lot for gases and liquids, which are physical things but not solid as we usually think of it. But let us go with the basic idea.

A spiritual substance, in contrast, is not extended in space, located, or impenetrable. Those are all physical attributes. A spiritual substance is not supposed to be in space at all, though some think of it as in time. Ghosts are sometimes depicted in movies as semi-transparent, suggesting that they are not really material. And they can pass through walls, so they are not impenetrable. Should they even be depicted as being at a place?

For Descartes, the essence of mind was *thought*. One's mind is a thinking thing, and it is this thinking thing that is supposed to be able to live on, disembodied. Now thoughts also seem to require no spatial attributes, which is what allows us to conceive of them without a body. Suppose you think that today is Tuesday and you also desire to own a Salvador Dali original painting. Is your desire to own a Dali to the left or to the right of your belief that it is Tuesday? Arguably, there is no sensible answer because beliefs are not characterized by a location.

Whether we live in a world that contains the mental and physical as distinct kinds of substance is thus one question, and an exemplary metaphysical one. Such a *dualism* is challenged by the view that we can explain everything in terms of just one type of substance. Materialists think that all mental things are reducible to material things. Idealists think that all material things are reducible to mental things. Everything about the one can be explained in terms of the other, on these views. But suppose one maintains that there are both: the material and immaterial. Then we would have a further problem of how the two interact.

When the spirit moves you

It seems clear, as physically embodied thinking things, that mind and body interact causally. The decisions you make in your mind affect what your body does and how it behaves. A decision to run for the bus makes your legs move. Recollection of an embarrassing incident makes you blush. And what happens to your body affects you mentally. If your body is injured, you feel pain. If your body is tired, your thinking becomes difficult and unreliable. And physical stimuli to your bodily senses cause you to perceive. According to the dualist, all our thoughts, sensations, and perceptions are within the sphere of the mental. A dualist doesn't have to accept that mind and body interact, but they have some explaining to do if they deny it.

The difficult question a dualist would have to face, therefore, is if mind and body are such distinct kinds of thing, how are they able to affect each other? The descriptions of the mental and physical given above suggest that they are of such different natures that causation between them looks out of the question. When a physical thing causes another physical thing, such as a kick causing a ball to move, one thing presses into another. There is movement or momentum transferred from the kick to the ball. We think of causation as a physical process. But mental or spiritual things do not have location in space, nor extension, nor solidity. So how could a movement of something solid affect them? Where would such a transaction go on? What would there be to stop the physical movement going straight through the mental substance, just like those movie ghosts?

This is the problem of mind–body interaction, and it is such a difficult one that some dualists have been prepared to say that, contrary to appearance, the mind and its body do not interact, after all. Another response would be to say that we need a different concept of causation to explain the interaction. If we restrict the concept of causation to physical causation, then of course it won't apply to spiritual substances.

There are nevertheless some who have thought this problem insurmountable. I mentioned that one view is to explain all mental things in terms of the physical. Perhaps the mind is nothing more than brain processes. This need not be an all-out reduction of the mental to the physical: claiming that pain, for instance, is just a certain type of brain process or that the belief that today is Tuesday is a certain pattern of neuron firings. It is unlikely that the complexities of the mind can be accounted for in terms of simple types of physical events like those. But the physicalist will say that ultimately some such kind of explanation exists for the mind, even if the details would be staggeringly complex. Here, we might recall the issues discussed in Chapter 3.

Is consciousness just the product of physical parts arranged in the right way, or is there something else about it: something emergent?

Rather than run that same discussion again, there is something more about persons and that needs to be discussed. To qualify as a person, following Locke, it was suggested that one needs a sufficiently sophisticated mental life, capable of experiencing sensations, thinking, and acting. Whether this is ultimately explicable physically is not the concern. But we should consider again the view that what makes someone the same person now as the person they were in the past is psychological continuity. The problem is the one we encountered in Chapter 1 concerning numerical identity. In this case, it is what makes a person at one time the very same person at a later time.

Two into one won't go

Psychological continuity is a fine idea, but it has a problem that it is not necessarily a one-to-one relation, whereas we think that identity, including personal identity, is. By this, we mean that a person in the year 2012 can be identical with at most one person in 2002 (if they had been born by then). Similarly, the 2012 person can be identical with at most one person in 2022 (assuming they live until then). For any person at any time, there will be at most one person with whom they are identical at any other time.

However, we see that a person at a certain time could have psychological continuity with a number of people at other times. How so? Here's an example. In an old 1960s episode of the original *Star Trek*, 'The Enemy Within', Captain Kirk gets split in two due to a transporter mechanism failure. Both the 'new' Kirks that emerge can remember graduating from Starfleet Academy. They both recall their request for Scotty to beam them up. Somehow, the transporter duplicated Kirk in every detail: both bodily and psychologically. This is, of course, the stuff of science fiction but it seems a logical possibility. All that matters for philosophers is that it could be true. In the *Star Trek* story, the two Kirks are actually a bit different. One gets all the badness and aggression, and the other gets all the niceness and indecision. But they are equally close to the original Kirk, and we could imagine a case where the two new Kirks are the same. Towards the end of the episode, the two have a fight and argue 'I'm Kirk!'; 'No, I'm Kirk', and that sort of thing.

This puts the psychological account of personal identity in some difficulty. It seems that neither new Kirk is identical to the old one, because there are two of them and only one of him. Identity is one–one. And yet, suppose after the first one had come back as before, Scotty had seen that the malfunctioning transporter was in the process of creating another. Realizing that having two Kirks would mean the original Kirk effectively ceased to be, Scotty decides to destroy Kirk number two before the process of assembling him is complete.

On this second story, it seems that the post-transporter Kirk is identical with the original Kirk. He has adequate psychological continuity with the original, and there is only one of him. He has no one else to contest with him the identity of Kirk. And yet why should it matter so much whether some other person is around or not? Might we think that identity should be a matter intrinsic to the individual(s) concerned? Should it really depend on whether someone else exists? I am pretty sure I'm identical with the young man who graduated. Yet I cannot rule out the possibility that last night my bedroom was invaded by a mad scientist with a full brain and body scanner that created a duplicate of me elsewhere this morning. Given that I do not know for sure whether such a duplicate is being kept elsewhere, then I cannot know for sure whether I really am identical with the Huddersfield graduate of 1989.

8. **Could this machine split you in two?**

All in the mind?

So far, I have been willing to run with the idea that psychological continuity is the key thing, following Locke's original idea. But can we really trust in that account? If the mad scientist goes and creates a duplicate of you, can't you still claim to be the original, even if the duplicate has replicated your mind entirely? And here's how you could argue it. You are the real you because you are the original organism. As well as psychological continuity with the original, you can also point to bodily continuity. You woke up in the same bed you went to sleep in last night, and you did not leave it in between. There was a continuous line in space and time between you now and what was you throughout the past. There is no such line with the impostor. He was created in a shabby laboratory on the other side of town, more than 5 miles from where you lay. The poor soul may think he's you, but he's not. Pity him or her.

Here is another consideration in favour of this view. Suppose an American historian reads everything there is on J. F. Kennedy.

Perhaps he becomes the world's leading expert. But he works so hard at his academic career that he suffers a complete mental breakdown. He starts to believe that he is J. F. Kennedy and that he's only just woken up after a coma that began in November 1963. Because he knows so much about Kennedy's life, he can tell you all about everything 'he' has done. He tells you it all from a first-person perspective. In his delusion, he remembers being president during the Bay of Pigs calamity and the Cuban Missile Crisis.

This shows that Locke's memory criterion of personal identity is inadequate. We can distinguish between true and false memories where the false ones are in some way illusory. There are some cases where people hear stories so many times they start to believe that they witnessed them first hand when they didn't. Purported memory is not enough.

Assuming then that first-person testimony is not enough to make a memory real – or perhaps not enough for it to count as a memory as opposed to only a pseudo-memory – there must be some other basis on which we distinguish real and illusory memories. And what better a criterion than the physical continuity in space and time of the body? Our historian is not Kennedy because he has no bodily continuity with Kennedy. Kennedy's body still lies in Arlington cemetery, Virginia. The historian has never even been to Arlington. Indeed, while Kennedy was being killed in Dallas, our historian was a young boy in New York, and so on.

If we think of a bodily criterion of personal identity, it can release us from some of the problem cases that have been raised. But not all of them. In the *Star Trek* teleportation case, the two Kirks might have equal claim to physical as well as mental, psychological continuity with the original Kirk. It seems in principle possible that a person is split, amoeba-like, body and soul. Maybe we just have to admit that in such cases identity is lost.

What, then, is a person? Your answer will depend first on whether you think we are souls or not. If we are inextricably tied to a body, then psychological and physical factors seem crucial to what makes us what we are both at a time and also over time. But such continuity might not be enough in every case to determine personal identity.

Chapter 8
What is possible?

'I coulda been a contender' is one of the most famous lines in movie history (Marlon Brando in *On the Waterfront*, 1954). Could he really? We accept lots of things to be possible that are not actual. You could have been late to your appointment if there had been an incident on the way; Michael Foot could have been prime minister; the Eiffel Tower could have been disassembled in 1909, and it could have been 350 metres high, instead of its actual height. Yet we also accept that many things are not possible. You couldn't jump to the Moon; lead can't transmute into gold; a leopard can't turn into a chicken; and so on. There are some things that might be possible or might not, and we don't know which. We seek a cure for cancer, for example, and we don't yet quite know whether one is possible, though we hope so. Who would have thought when sticky black oil was first found in the ground that it would make motor-car propulsion possible? Science and technology often progress by discovering hitherto unknown possibilities within things.

What are these possibilities? Are they a part of the reality that we have been cataloguing? We have found particulars, their properties, changes, causes, so what about possibilities? Are they things? Do they have any kind of being? Or are they a mere fabrication: things we can think about but which are not really a part of the furniture of the world?

Before addressing those questions, we need a clarification. The possibilities considered here are those that are possible but without being actual. It is necessary to say this so that the answer to our question is not trivial. All that is actual is of course possible: for how else could it be actual? So those possibilities are real enough. No dispute there. That London is the capital city of England is both possible and actual, so certainly a part of reality. That Winchester was the capital until 1066 may be a part of reality depending on your view of facts about the past (see Chapter 6). But some really interesting metaphysical questions arise when we consider those possibilities that are not also actual. We can distinguish such non-actual possibilities by calling them 'mere' possibilities. Lincoln escaping assassination in 1865 is a mere possibility, as is Wayne Rooney succeeding David Cameron as prime minister and Beeston being the current capital of England. You are likely to get tired of me using the word 'mere', however, so I will just say now that when I discuss possibilities, I mean those that are non-actual.

Coulda, woulda, shoulda

The key question, then, is whether such things are real or not. In a way, they are clearly not. If you see a sign by the road saying 'Possible queues ahead', and you know that it is a mere possible queue, then you have nothing to fear, for only an actual queue can delay you. The idea that Beeston could now be the capital city matters not at all. And although the Eiffel Tower could have been 350 metres high, an air balloon passing over it needn't consider this but only its actual height.

Then again, it seems foolish to ignore possibilities if they could become actual. There's a possibility of skin cancer if you stay in the sun regularly and for too long, and a possibility of lung cancer if you smoke. Surely you shouldn't ignore these possibilities. And when a glass is fragile, it means it could break relatively easily. This should determine how you handle it, assuming you don't want it breaking. Every time you drive a car down the motorway, there is any number of possible crashes awaiting you if you were to be careless. You should take care precisely to avoid making them actual. The possibilities that surround us do indeed seem to shape the way we interact with the world and, on that basis, seem to have some reality.

Maybe there are two types of possibility, then. That the Eiffel Tower could have been 350 metres high – or 450 metres high even – seems of no real consequence. Only its actual height affects the way we should behave towards it: if trying to get over it in a hot-air balloon, for instance. But other possibilities are of consequence, where our behaviour could easily bring them about. And although we want to avoid bringing about car crashes through recklessness, there are many other possibilities we aim to achieve. It's possible to be rich, or learned, or athletically excellent, and many people strive to make these things so.

We have already encountered an idea (in Chapter 5) that many people find useful in understanding what possibilities are. When we considered causation, we saw the theory that in some other

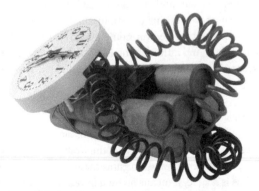

9. What is possible here?

possible world an event that occurs in our world does not occur in that one. The notion of a possible world has a broader use than just accounting for causation, however. There is also an idea that when we think of a possibility, we are thinking of something that does occur or is a fact at another world. Hence, there is another world in which Michael Foot was prime minister and another, not necessarily the same one, in which the Eiffel Tower is 350 metres tall. In another, Lincoln survived assassination and died of old age. On this account, every possibility of our world is actual at some other world; so there are as many worlds as there are possibilities, which sounds like an awful lot.

But what are these other worlds? Are they a part of reality? First of all, by a possible world, we don't mean something like a planet. In old science-fiction stories, we may refer to other planets as worlds, but the idea here is that a world is a whole universe. Our world – the actual one – encompasses everything there is. That would be the whole of space and time complete with its occupants: the properties, particulars, changes, and causes that make up the entirety of which we are a part. And the other worlds are supposed to be just like that too, complete with their planets and stars, people, trivial facts, tables and chairs, prime ministers, and capital cities. Some possible worlds will have no life in them at all, however, and while some will be vast universes, others will be very small. There's even a possible world that contains just two objects sitting in a spatially symmetrical relationship (we came across this world already in Chapter 1).

In other worlds

Opinion divides from this point on. It may be a surprise to hear that there is a view in which all these worlds are just as real as ours. They exist in the fullest sense of the word, in exactly the same way that our world exists. Just as the table in front of you is a physical object that makes a noise when you bang it, there are physical tables in other possible worlds that can make a noise when they are banged too. Some worlds are even inhabited in places by people: not necessarily human beings but things capable of thinking and acting (in still other worlds, remarkably, these persons are computers). These people can feel sensations just like we do, and they can think about whether there are other possible worlds like theirs. You can even have counterparts in some of these worlds: people who look very like you, with a similar history, and they may even have the same name as you.

Although these worlds are real, however, we can never visit them. They are within space and time, with physical occupants, which is why they are sometimes called *concrete* possible worlds. But they are not within *our* space and time. Every world is spatiotemporally separated from every other world. Indeed, this could be part of what we mean by a world. If something is spatiotemporally connected to our world, it is thereby a part of our world; for you could in theory get there. And in this metaphysic, it should be clear that while we use the term *actual* to refer to our world, occupants of other worlds use the term to refer to their own. *Actual* thus becomes an indexical term, like *I*, *we*, *here*, and *now*. The reference of such terms varies according to who uses it. When I say *here*, it refers to Nottingham, but, when you use it, it refers to Oslo, Istanbul, St Louis, Antigonish, or wherever you are.

When David Lewis (in *Counterfactuals*, 1973, and then in *On the Plurality of Worlds*, 1986) first proposed this realism about possible worlds, his account was met with incredulous stares. Yes, he really did mean that reality was packed with an infinite number of concrete worlds of which ours was just one. But an incredulous stare is not an argument. One reaction was to say something along the following lines. When we speak of the possibility that the Eiffel Tower is 350 metres high, we could think of that as meaning it has that height in another possible world, but we shouldn't treat such a world as real. It's a merely possible world, not a real one. So perhaps we can use possible worlds as a conceptual aid in articulating our thoughts about possibility. Such worlds would be *abstract* only. By saying something is possible, we can say that there's a possible world in which it's true, but we don't mean this literally. We could accept the language of possible worlds without being committed to them as a metaphysical reality.

Lewis was dismissive of such 'ersatz' realism, however. One thing he was trying to do was analyse what it is for something to be possible. His answer was that there was a concrete world in which that thing was true. Such worlds were as real as ours. If we try to resist this last step, then we cannot do what Lewis was trying to do. We cannot analyse what a possibility is because all we can say about these other worlds is that they are possible, rather than Lewis's which are all actual worlds. To say that for something to be *possible* is for it to be true at a *possible* world, is to provide a circular, uninformative account. We should not, therefore, look to downgrade such worlds; if we do, then they may be unable to perform the substantial task for which they were intended. Such a line of argument might not be the end of the matter, however.

The motivation to back away from Lewis's strong realism about possibilities is understandable, however. He makes them as much a part of reality as anything. They are just not a part of the little corner of reality that we call home. They are someone else's home. Reality becomes a much bigger thing than we might have thought, therefore. We could think of this as rather metaphysically cumbersome. There must be a world for every single possibility, so our own world is an infinitesimally small part of the totality. Do we really need this much just to account for possibility? Philosophers are not very economical, are they?

Again, though, this is not an argument. There is no reason why the most economical theory should be true. The world (or all of them) could be a messy place where the truth of the matter is complex and involves a great many things. But here is a consideration that might be a bit more serious (opinions on its significance vary greatly). The statement with which we began was 'I coulda been a contender'. Note the emphasis on *I*. Many of the claims we make about possibility refer to particulars. The Eiffel Tower could have been 350 metres tall, Lincoln could have survived assassination, and I could have been a professional footballer. But if realism about possible worlds is true, these claims about possibility, strictly speaking, are not.

According to the theory, what it is for it to be true that I could have been a footballer is that there is another world containing someone who is a lot like me, my counterpart, who is a footballer. But what do I care about this other guy? He's not me; indeed, he's not part of my world at all. Nothing he says or does can affect me because worlds cannot causally interact. So, in a sense, I couldn't have been a footballer, after all, if I follow the implications of the theory. Only some other guy was. Similarly, the Eiffel Tower of our world is 324 metres tall. We think it could have been 350 metres tall, but the theory tells us only that there is another world containing a counterpart of the Eiffel Tower that is 350 metres tall. What does this tell us about our world and the tower within it? It couldn't have been 350 metres, given that it is in fact 324 metres. All the theory says is that it's like some other tower that is 350 metres tall. This looks like quite a big letdown of the theory. In establishing realism about worlds, in order to tell us what possibility is, it seems to have had the opposite effect because it restricts us to differences occurring to counterparts of our world's inhabitants. Brando wanted to know whether *he* could have been a contender, and we wonder whether *our* Eiffel Tower could have been dismantled in 1909. The realist about possible worlds has some work to do to answer this criticism.

Combinations and recombinations

The possible worlds account is not the only game in town, however. It is worth looking at another. We might think of this second account as more Aristotelian than Platonic. Let us suppose that mere possibilities have no existence whatsoever. Nevertheless, there seems to be something to them. How can we account for them? It has been suggested that we could think of possibilities as recombinations of all the existing elements in reality.

Here's how it could work. Suppose you are fairly new to the world with only a limited experience. One minute a white dog walks by. The next minute you see a black cat. You now know that there are these two kinds of particulars: a dog and a cat. But you also know that there are two properties as well: whiteness and blackness. Although you've seen only a white dog and a black cat, you now see that a black dog and a white cat are also possible. All you have done is rearrange in your head the existing elements. You have seen which particulars exist and which properties; and you have just redistributed or rearranged them. Similarly, you know that there are various buildings in the world, and you know that there are various height properties. 350 metres is not the height of the Eiffel Tower, but given that you know that the Eiffel Tower exists and that 350 metres is a height, then you can put those two elements together in your mind and think of a possible 350-metre-high Eiffel Tower.

The possibilities have some kind of existence: but only in so far as the elements exist out of which they are built. The recombinations that are merely possible have no concrete existence. The 350-metre Eiffel Tower is a mere fiction. The tower exists, and the height, but not their combination. That is the thing that is merely imagined.

We need not require that someone does the actual imagining, however, or write the fiction. For something to be possible, it can suffice just that the particular and the property exist that would, if they were combined, constitute it. They could form a recombination that no one ever thinks of. Abraham Lincoln is a particular, for instance, and there is such an activity (or property) as scuba diving. So Abraham Lincoln scuba diving is a possibility even if no one ever mentions it. It has now been mentioned here, but there are lots of other possibilities that no one has ever mentioned nor thought of.

This theory of possibility was developed by David Armstrong (*A Combinatorial Theory of Possibility*, 1989). We can think of all the world's elements in the form of a grid. Arrange all the particulars on one axis and all the properties on the other. A particular apple would be one particular, and greenness one of the properties, but there will be many more besides. We could think of some of the grid spaces where a certain property and a certain particular intersect as filled in (with a tick, perhaps). This would indicate that the property was held by that particular. It would be a fact, for instance, that this apple is green. But many of the spaces would be left blank. Abraham Lincoln was not green, so there would be no need to tick that box. If we discover all the spaces that are ticked on our grid, then we would have discovered all the facts about our world. We could have total knowledge. But the grid also tells us, on this theory, what all the mere possibilities are. They are all the blank spaces: all the boxes that are not ticked. Lincoln could have been green. This just means that Lincoln is a particular and greenness is a property.

This is a simple idea. As always, the devil's in the detail. This combinatorial account only works if you allow that the elements are recombinable. The principle of recombination – that any particular can be matched with any property – is doing all the work, one might think. And one could then wonder whether the combinatorial grid really tells us what the possibilities are or just assumes them by adopting the principle of free recombination.

One might wonder whether this principle should in any case be supported. Could Lincoln really have been green? Surely that is not a possible colour for human beings. Maybe there are at least some restrictions on what is possible. It was remarked earlier that you couldn't jump to the Moon, but on this account it seems this might count as a possibility. You exist, and there is a property of jumping to the Moon, so that seems to be possible unless we impose some restrictions.

Distinctions are often made between types of possibility. There is that which is logically possible, meaning simply that it would not involve a contradiction or violate the laws of logic. And there is natural possibility: what the laws of nature permit. The latter include laws of physics, biology, chemistry, sociology, optics, and so on. One could say that it is logically possible that Lincoln be green even if it is not a biological possibility. The natural possibilities would be some subset of the many more things that are logically possible. Hence we could allow unrestricted recombination to account for the logical possibilities and impose restrictions if we are talking about the natural ones.

The combinatorial theory of possibility can be criticized along these lines for allowing too much to be possible. But it also faces an objection from the opposite direction. It is not always able to deliver enough possibilities. The theory constructs possibilities out of recombinations of all the existing elements. But there is a thought that there might have been a bit more than there actually is. It seems a possibility that there might have been one more particular or one more property. Kennedy could have had an extra child, for instance, instead of the four he actually had. It seems a possibility but not a recombination of what there is. The extra child I'm imagining is a whole other extra particular: another element there would have to be in reality. The theory can protect a little bit against this objection but not completely. One could couple it with a four-dimensional view, which would give you all the particulars and properties there ever was and ever will be and leave them all available for recombination. But even if the number of elements is huge, it is still finite. There could still, we feel, have been more: such as that unborn child.

One who adopts the possible worlds account, on the other hand, can say simply that there are worlds that contain more than ours does. There would be a world in which Kennedy indeed has a fifth child. We should not forget the problem with that account, however. The man with five children in the other world is not Kennedy, and the fifth child is not an unborn one of this world. We have two main theories of possibility, therefore, and both have their weaknesses. You may have noticed a pattern of inconclusiveness by now. Such is often the way in our discipline, but it does show that there is plenty of work left to do for all the possible future philosophers.

Chapter 9
Is nothing something?

We have been considering what there is and what it is. It made sense to start with the easy things. It seemed clear that there were particulars and properties, that changes occurred and some of them could be caused. There were wholes as well as parts, and there were persons. Some other topics were less easy. It is disputed whether wholes are sometimes more than their parts, what possibilities are, whether spiritual substances exist, and whether time is a thing that passes.

The next category of thing looks more suspicious than any of the above. Nevertheless, it is not easy to dismiss out of hand. There seems to be a class of rather shady alleged entities: the nothingnesses. There are absences, lacks, edges, emptinesses, limits, holes, zeros, missings, voids, and endings, which all seem to be various kinds of nothing. The cheese contains a hole, for instance. Is the hole part of the cheese? Is it something that can be contained? Is it any kind of entity at all? The cheese itself seems real enough, but maybe the hole is nothing at all: just an empty space. The extent of the hole is the boundary of the cheese. Yet even a boundary seems to entail some kind of nothingness. It's the limit of the cheese – its end – beyond which there is none. It is the edge between being and non-being.

Nothing ventured, nothing gained

Philosophers have been deeply divided on the subject of nothings, absences, and so on. Some have been prepared to invoke them, and indeed allow them some degree of reality of being. We often say things like 'there is no food in the cupboard', which superficially looks to be ascribing existence ('there is ...') to something negative ('no food ...'). An initial reaction might be to say that such words are clearly not meant to be taken that way. But the problem is that absence-talk is very hard to eliminate. We invoke nothings all the time, and it is far from clear that we can explain them in terms of the 'positive' things that we know to exist. For this reason, some philosophers have come to take absences seriously, permitting them as part of reality. They may be a full part of reality or they may have only a partial existence. They may be second-class citizens of our world. A rejoinder to this latter option is the thought that existence is univocal: something either exists or it doesn't, and there is nothing in between.

This most perplexing of subjects might become clearer as we start to consider examples, though in doing so, we will see that the cases are not so easily dismissed. Earlier, we considered the question 'What is a circle?', and this led us to consider properties. A man may have the property of being 1.8 metres tall. Does that mean he also has the property of being not-2.0 metres tall? Do things have negative properties as well as their positive ones? A shape-card may have the properties of being triangular and red. Does it also have the properties of being not-square and not-blue? There seems something dubious about such negative properties, but what exactly? Is there any principled basis we could have for ruling them out?

There are a couple of thoughts we might have. In the first place, you could argue that if things had negative properties, they would have to have an infinite number of them. Given that a man has the 'positive' property of being 1.8 metres tall, then if we allowed him to have the 'negative' property of being not-2.0 metres tall, we would also have to allow him the properties of being not-2.1 metres, not-2.2 metres, not-2.3 metres, and so on for every possible height. Similarly, if we said our red triangular card had the property of being not-blue, we would also have to say it had the properties of not-green, not-pink, not-orange, as well as not-circular, not-trapezium, and so on for every colour and shape. But how compelling is that point? It is an objection that if we allow negative properties, it would entail that things have an infinite number of properties. But are we sure that's not the case anyway? How many properties does the room have in which you are sitting? Look around. Are you really sure the number is finite? In which case, this might not be a good enough argument against the existence of negative properties, after all.

Here is another argument. If two people are 1.8 metres tall, they have something in common. They share a property. There is a *One* – a unity – that runs through this *Many.* But if two people are not-2.0 metres tall, it would seem that they need have nothing in common at all regarding their height. Mary could be not-2.0 metres in virtue of being 1.6 metres tall. John could be not-2.0 metres in virtue of being 1.9 metres. There is no shared property, therefore. No One running through Many. But this argument also falls short. The problem is that it's question-begging. Only if one has already decided that negative properties are not genuine would it work. If someone wanted to defend negative properties, they could simply assert that Mary and John do indeed have something in common: they are both not-2.0 metres tall.

There is another thought, perhaps more serious. Given that someone is 1.8 metres tall, we could say that all the other heights that they are not are simply entailed by this. Rather than suggesting that this person has a property of being not-2.0 metres, one can simply deduce it as a mere fact or truth from the positive property that they do have. Perhaps, then, one needn't invoke a separate realm of negative properties. They are merely entailed facts derived from all the positive ones.

Again, there are problems, though. How does being 1.8 metres tall entail being not-2.0 metres? Arguably, it does so because being 1.8 metres is incompatible with being 2.0 metres. But an incompatibility looks like another kind of negative. The incompatibility is that nothing can be both 1.8 metres and 2.0 metres. Have we just, therefore, swapped one kind of negative existence for another? Do we want to allow that incompatibilities are part of reality?

And would an incompatibility strategy always work anyway? The room you are in, I assume, has the property of not containing a hippopotamus. But I also assume there could be one. It could fit in. None of the positive properties of the room entail that it's not-hippopotamus-containing. It's just that it doesn't have such a property.

Should we permit negative properties, then, or stick with our intuition that they are dubious? There are two more cases to discuss before attempting an answer. I take these first because all the cases may permit a common response.

Causation by absence has been taken seriously even by philosophers of high repute, despite its absurdity. What is causation by absence? Consider the case where you go on holiday and come home to find your plants dead. What killed them? Absence of water, you might think. There are many cases like this where the absence of something – which sounds a great deal like a nothingness – nevertheless seems to be causally active. Absence of oxygen can kill humans by suffocation, lack of insulin production is the cause of diabetes, a horseshoe comes loose for want of a nail, and machines usually fail if a part is taken out. There are also some causal mechanisms that work precisely through absences. A car airbag, for instance, works when the force of a sudden stop is strong enough for a magnetic ball bearing to break free of the top of a metal pipe, in through which air can rush. The crash causes the airbag to deploy only through the absence of this ball bearing.

The idea of causation by absence starts to look attractive when you consider these cases. Yet to grant that absences have causal powers looks metaphysically dangerous. In the first place, many would take causal efficacy as a good criterion of something being real. So if we allow that absences can causally affect things, then it would look as if we are allowing them full existence. We would have to reify (treat as real) absences. The stakes are high. And if we allow that absences can be causes, it seems that the causes of any event would proliferate to the point of absurdity.

Here's an example (due to Phil Dowe) that illustrates the point. Had a security guard thrown their body in the way of the bullet, Kennedy would have lived. If you think absences can be causes, it seems that you have to say that one of the causes of Kennedy's death was the absence of this security guard. But, then again, if Jack Ruby had thrown his body in the way, Kennedy would have lived. Not just the absence of the security guard but also the absence of Jack Ruby would then have to be causes of his death. But if you or I had been in the way of the bullet, we could have saved Kennedy. Indeed, any human who ever has or ever will exist could also have stopped the bullet. So among the causes of Kennedy's death are the absences of every person. And we don't have to stop there. Inanimate objects could also have stopped the bullet. Clearly, therefore, Kennedy's death would have been caused by a limitless number of such absences. Do we want to allow the number of causes of an event to escalate in this way? Shouldn't we take it as a sign that something has gone wrong with our account?

Exactly what has gone wrong is not easy to pin down, however. We have a similar problem to the case of negative properties. Maybe an event does have an infinite number of causes. And the absence does seem to play a crucial role in some causal explanations. It is

10. What caused this?

specifically the absence of oxygen that asphyxiates people, rather than absence of rubber chickens or anything else. Can one say that the absence of oxygen is entailed by the presence of other things? That doesn't look easy to do. In that case, an absence may be an essential feature of the causal situation, which doesn't look good for our positive metaphysics.

It's only words

The thought that nothing is nothing but a word is a tempting one. It would be very neat metaphysically if all these absences and nothingnesses could be confined to language: a feature of the way we speak, rather than something that is part of the world. Is there hope in that direction? There may be, but it depends on one's view of the relation between the world, language, and truth.

When you say 'there is not a hippopotamus in this room', you may well claim that this is perfectly harmless. You are not invoking a property of non-hippopotamus-containing, you might argue, and you are certainly not claiming that there are negative objects. One would not want to say that as well as containing the 'positive' objects of a table and chair, the room also contained the 'negative' object non-hippopotamus. You are merely asserting, you might declare, that there is no 'positive', real, existing hippo here.

This would be fine if it worked, but some think that it doesn't. When I say truly that there is a table in the room, it strikes me that there is something in the world in virtue of which my statement is true. What makes it true is that there is indeed a table – a physical object – contained inside the four walls of my room. My statement is a kind of linguistic entity that is capable of truth or falsehood. What determines which (true or false) seems to be whether or not there is something in the world that makes it true. Sometimes more than one thing can make a statement true. I say that there is also a chair in my room. In fact, there are several and each one is sufficient for the truth of the statement that there is a chair in my room. So far, this sounds plausible. But what of a statement like 'there is not a hippopotamus in my room'? What is it that makes this kind of negative statement true? What are the worldly truthmakers for the negative truths?

Again, seemingly sane philosophers have in some way reified absences to explain the problem. Bertrand Russell (*Lectures on Logical Atomism*, 1918) wrestled with this issue and could see no option but to accept that the world contained negative facts as well as positive ones, for only the former, he thought, could explain negative truths.

We have already encountered the reasons why Russell would say this. One might try to argue that when we state a negative truth, we are really just asserting a different, 'positive' truth that is incompatible with the opposite of our statement. This is the sort of situation in which philosophy requires mental gymnastics. If you say 'Fred is not-2.0 metres tall', it's suggested that you are really asserting the positive truth that Fred is actually 1.7 metres tall, and being 1.7 metres tall is incompatible with being 2.0 metres tall. But, first, it's implausible that this is what you're doing. Fred may be 1.7 metres tall, but you might not know that. All you see is that he's not 2.0 metres tall (perhaps he walks under a 2.0-metre bar without bending). Second, as we've seen, even if this were what you were saying, it would be swapping one negative for another. I would be asserting Fred is 1.7 metres tall, and that being 1.7 metres is incompatible with being 2.0 metres. An incompatibility is a negative: it is not the case that anything is both 1.7 metres tall and 2.0 metres tall. And, third, in the hippopotamus case, it's hard to see what its presence in the room is supposed to be incompatible with. As mentioned above, there's nothing stopping it being there: it could easily walk in. It's just that it's not there.

We sometimes think of a fact to mean a true statement. But there is also a metaphysical concept of a fact, which is that of a particular bearing a property, where both elements are needed. Hence the fact of the apple being round is a different fact from the fact of the apple being red. The room containing a hippopotamus would also count as a fact. Because Russell saw no other solution to the problem of negative truth, he was willing to allow that there are also negative facts. So it could be a fact – as much a part of reality as anything – that the room contains no hippopotamus. There could be a fact that the apple is not green, and another that Fred is not-2.0 metres tall. Another way of putting this might be to say that Fred negatively instantiates the property of being 2.0 metres, where negatively instantiating a property is the opposite of instantiating one. Either way, some kind of negative element is being allowed into existence.

Much ado about nothing

That is one way to go. We could allow negative facts, absences as causes, negative properties, and the like. On the other hand, we could return to the thought that negation is a feature of language rather than of the world. If I say that I have nothing in my pocket, surely no one thinks that it means I have something in my pocket, namely *the nothing*. To think that would be to almost wilfully misinterpret things. If I have nothing, I really do have nothing. The mistake of treating this nothing as if it were something seems very obvious in this case, but less so in the more intricate cases of truth, causation, and properties. But it also seems obvious that the bullet killed Kennedy, not the absence of a truck driving between the sniper and his victim.

The view that nothingness is all in our heads might go something like this. There is one reality and everything that exists is 'positive'. There are no negative entities, properties, or causes. We as conscious subjects of experience can think about our world. When we do so, we can think about it in two separate ways. We can think about what is, and we can make assertions about it. But we can also deny things of the world. If asked whether there's a hippopotamus in my room, I deny it. When I assert something, I am making a statement about how the world is; but that's not what I'm doing when I deny something. When I deny that Fred is 2.0 metres tall, I'm not asserting that he is any particular height, I am rather denying that he is that particular height.

Not everyone in philosophy likes the talk of truthmakers, but for those who do, we can note an important asymmetry between assertion and denial. When I assert something, I am committed to the existence of its truthmaker. To say there is a chair in the room is to commit to there being a fact in the world that makes the statement true: the fact that a certain kind of physical object sits within the room. If there is no such fact, then the statement is wrong. But with denial, there is no commitment to the existence of anything. Now if I say 'Jimmy is not tall', I may commit to the existence of something. Opinion divides on this. I may be committing to Jimmy's existence. But the negative part of the statement contains no commitment. I deny of Jimmy that he is tall. I need nothing to make my denial true because it is not saying that the world is a certain way: it's denying that it is.

We bring our denials to bear across a range of situations. Jean-Paul Sartre discussed the case of entering a restaurant and seeing that Pierre is absent. How can anyone do that? Absences can't be perceived directly, for how would the absence of Pierre look any different from the absence of Jacques or the absence of a hippopotamus? Absent things look like nothing so, in that respect, they are indistinguishable. It seems problematic to say that the absence of Pierre is inferred from what is seen because, just like the hippopotamus case, there is nothing you see that entails he's not there. It's just that he's not. The judgement might be of a primitive, non-deductive kind, then. We just have an ability to judge that something is not, which is denying that it is. You deny that Pierre is in the room because you've had a good look around and, try as you might, you couldn't find him.

It is to be hoped that we could say similar things about the other cases in which absences seem to play a role. One may see that if an object had been in the way of a bullet, it could have stopped it. But that is very far from saying that the absence of that object caused someone's death. That would again be bringing something into physical existence that is best understood as a way of thinking. And, as already intimated, we can make all sorts of judgements about the way the world is not – that Fred is not 2.0 metres tall, for instance – but that should not lead us to think that there is some kind of negative fact about the world that makes such thoughts true. The thought wasn't about the way the world was; it was about a way the world wasn't.

The subject of nothing is one of the most difficult in the whole of metaphysics. It is a tangle. The philosopher's job is sometimes to disentangle things. After that has been done, we may hope it would show that nothingnesses, absences, lacks, and so on, are no part of existence. They would be so much trouble if they were.

Chapter 10
What is metaphysics?

Now that we have looked at some of the main questions discussed
in metaphysics, we are in a better informed position to answer the
question of what metaphysics is. Metaphysics is the activity we
have been doing in the previous nine chapters. Having engaged in
it, we are in a better position to understand it.

Many of the questions will have sounded simple, silly, or childish,
and they are often dismissed as such. Once we grow up, we are not
expected to ask what a circle is, whether time passes, or whether
nothing is something. It is almost as if the natural sense of wonder
with which we are born is disciplined out of us.

Perhaps metaphysics is thought of as a useless waste of time or,
even worse, a dangerous distraction. We shouldn't forget the story
(probably only half true) that Socrates was put to death for being
such an annoyance. The reader will have seen, however, that these
very simple questions can lead to complicated answers. Just from
asking what a circle is, we quickly got into some deep issues about
the nature of the world, reality, and what exists. Pondering on
such issues may have helped develop our minds. We have had to
think quite hard and perform some mental acrobatics. But is
metaphysics any more use than that? We have gained
understanding, perhaps, but it looks like there is no use to which

we can put that understanding. The charge of pointlessness seems to stand.

What have we been doing in these past nine chapters, then? One answer is that we have been trying to understand the fundamental nature of reality. But it is only one aspect of reality that we have been interested in, and only one kind of understanding that we have sought. Science also seeks to understand the nature of reality, but it does so in a different way. Science looks for some general truths, but they are also concrete, whereas the truths of metaphysics are very general and abstract.

When we consider what exists, the philosopher's answer will be at the highest levels of generality. They may say there are particulars that fall into natural kinds, there are properties, changes, causes, laws of nature, and so on. The job of science, however, is to say what specific things exist under each of those categories. There are electrons, for instance, or tigers, or chemical elements. There are properties of spin, charge, and mass, there are processes such as dissolution, there are laws of nature such as the law of gravitational attraction.

Metaphysics seeks to organize and systematize all these specific truths that science discovers and to describe their general features. Although, in explaining metaphysics, I have tried to use plenty of examples by way of illustration, the reader will also have seen that the choice was somewhat arbitrary. I asked what is a circle and what is a table. I could just as well have asked what is redness or what is a molecule. These were just ways of getting into the issues of properties in general and particulars in general.

Physics and metaphysics

There is a difference between metaphysics and science in the level of generality, but there is also a difference in approach. Although the disciplines have the same subject matter as their focus – the nature of the world – they seek to understand it from different directions. Science is based on observation, which is often its starting point and the ultimate arbiter of the truth of a theory. Metaphysics, while it's concerned with the world, is not so much concerned with that part of it that can be observed. What we can see with our eyes is of little help in metaphysics, or philosophy in general. The evidence of the senses is not what decides whether a philosophical theory is to be accepted or rejected.

We considered, for example, whether a table was just a bundle of properties or was a substance underlying and holding together all those properties. We should note that we cannot decide between these two theories on the basis of observation. The world would look the same whichever of them is true. It is not as if we could actually remove the properties of a real object and find a propertyless substratum. What would one look like, given that it was propertyless? Our questions are not, therefore, scientific ones. A difficulty students often have in starting metaphysics is that they cannot distinguish it from science, especially physics. They think that if the world is our subject matter, then we should look at the world and do so scientifically. We may use it for examples to get us started, but we cannot expect it to answer our metaphysical questions.

It may have been a historical accident that our discipline got its name. *Metaphysics* was the book of Aristotle's that came after the *Physics*. But, intended or not, there is another way of seeing the name that does describe the activity quite well. *Meta* can be interpreted to mean 'above' or 'beyond', and what we do in metaphysics is indeed above and beyond physics. It is above in its level of generality; and it is beyond the observational investigation of the world, thinking about the features that rationally the world should or could have. In that case, the discipline has a very suitable name indeed, because the problems discussed in Aristotle's book were precisely of this nature. It would also follow, however, that calling a practitioner of metaphysics a metaphysician is wrong. A physician is one who practises medicine. Our subject is not above and beyond medicine. A practitioner of physics is a physicist, and thus those who do metaphysics are metaphysicists.

Metaphysics has been challenged not just on the grounds that it is childish or annoying, however. When we concede that it is non-empirical – it's not about what can be observed with our senses – then there are many sceptics willing to attack it. If metaphysics is about something that cannot be observed, then how do we know anything about it and answer its questions? How do we know it is not all empty words or pure nonsense? Hume, and those who followed him, dismissed metaphysics on these grounds. Our ideas had to originate in our experience in order to have any meaning, the empiricist philosophers said. And if the terms used in metaphysics cannot be traced back to some original observation, then they are literally meaningless. Because of this, Hume recommended consigning metaphysics to the flames. He didn't see himself as a metaphysician, even though he has influenced many of the subsequent debates. Few have followed his suggestion of burning books, but Hume's critique has frequently resurfaced in more modern guises, such as in logical positivism.

One response to Hume was Kant's version of metaphysics in his *Critique of Pure Reason* (1781). This is depicted as a defence of metaphysics, but it is also possible to interpret Kant as somewhat lowering the ambitions of the subject. Kant scholars disagree on how best to understand him, but one way is to see his metaphysics as a description of the structure of our thinking about the world, rather than being about the world itself. Because of the limits of our thinking and experience, we must understand it in a certain way. Running with this idea, one might say that we have to think of the world in terms of particulars and their properties, or as being located in time and space, or as involving causes. Or one might say that metaphysics is just about the concepts that we use in describing the world and how they relate to each other. Perhaps metaphysics of this ilk is easier to defend, but it has to be acknowledged that it changes its nature fundamentally. Metaphysicists want to discover what the world is like, not the facts about our concepts, or about our psychology, or about only that part of the world that our psychology accommodates. Whether Kant's own position warrants this response is something I wouldn't dare comment upon. The point to make, however, is that it is tempting when metaphysics is under attack to retreat to some ground that is easier to defend. In doing so, however, it may no longer be metaphysics that is being defended.

Can we describe the practice of metaphysics in the pure original form and defend it against the attack that it is meaningless, useless, and pointless? The reader might consider whether the problems they have encountered over the past nine chapters have been meaningless. Perhaps you have the same intuition as me.

11. Immanuel Kant (1724–1804)

Although they are not settled through observation, it can still be claimed that they are genuine and meaningful questions. We can also contend that they are about the nature of the world, rather than just concepts or the way we think. Let us see if we can defend this view.

Seeing is believing?

To begin with, let us acknowledge that the powers of observation have been greatly exaggerated. Although scientists may use their senses, observation does not settle everything. What we believe in science is theoretical to a large extent. In that case, perhaps metaphysics is continuous with science. What metaphysicists do is not outlandishly different from what everyone else does who wants to understand the world. Metaphysics is at the more abstract and theoretical end of the scale, but it looks like more of a sliding scale than there being a very sharp boundary between the two disciplines.

In metaphysics, we have our thinking, our reasoning, as our guide to how the world could be or how it should be. We can reject accounts of some feature of the world if they are absurd, either by being counterintuitive or outright contradictory. The latter is preferable. A theory may entail that the world is some way but also not that way, in which case we would have grounds to reject that theory as incoherent. It may be rare that things are so clear cut, however. And even if they were, the defender of the theory might try to explain away the contradiction. More often, we would challenge a theory for saying or entailing something implausible. If one says that time flows, for instance, then it seems that one ought to be able to state the rate at which it flows. But we saw that this could not be meaningfully answered: it would trivially have to flow at one second per second. We also considered the theory that absences could be causes, but this also produced an absurd consequence. We would have to allow that a nothing could nevertheless have causal powers and, as we saw, that among the

103

causes of any event would be the absence of anything that could have prevented it.

When a consequence is so counterintuitive, we say that we have reduced the theory to absurdity. In the case of substance, it looked like we had reduced to absurdity the theory that a particular was a bundle of properties. There couldn't be, within that theory, two particulars with all the same properties, and there seems no good reason why we should accept this. There are, of course, philosophers who think the theory can avoid this *reductio ad absurdum*, so it is never the absolute end of the matter. And others might deny that such a consequence really is absurd. Nor should we assume that the truth of the matter always will be intuitive. We sometimes have to follow the argument and accept all it entails, even if it's surprising. There is always room for further philosophical debate, therefore.

Nothing here really hinged on the use of the senses. Certainly, you need to be a thinking thing to even get started in philosophy, and experiencing the world seems a precondition of that. Your senses probably also showed you that particularity was a feature of the world that needed explaining. It looks like there are particular things. But after that, it was down to your thinking in the abstract what a particular must be, or a cause, or time. You can explore the various theories, as fully as needs be. Some of them do not stand up to scrutiny.

Provisionally, we can reject some of the theories if it looks as though they have an intractable problem: if they seem to involve a contradiction or other absurdity. We accept that the problem may be overcome at some future point. So far, it doesn't look as if what the metaphysicist is doing is that much different from what some of the cleverest scientists do. A theoretical physicist might reject theories on similar grounds. There is one difference. Metaphysicists reject theories on the basis of reasoning alone: where the problem of the theory is one of internal coherence or contradiction with some other set of theories that we hold dear. In the case of sciences, the conflict that is the basis for rejecting a theory may be with some observational evidence. Science wants the theory to fit the observational facts, whereas the data of metaphysics are non-observational.

So far, this looks defensible. Metaphysics does not look conspicuously any less defensible than science. But, it might be argued, this is because we have only looked at the negative case in which a theory is rejected. Of course, a theory should be rejected if it is self-contradictory or leads to absurdity, whether it is in science or philosophy. But that only gives us grounds for ruling out theories, not for accepting them. And here it might be thought that science has the upper hand because it can find empirical confirmation of its theories. In philosophy, it is conceivable and very likely to be the case that there is more than one coherent theory about some issue. Multiple theories could be true individually even if they couldn't all be true at once. So how do we decide which one is right? Perhaps there is no truth in metaphysics, just a bunch of theories between which we cannot choose.

This again ignores the way that we think in both philosophy and in science. As we know from the philosophy of science, it is problematic to state simply that we know which theory of the world is true, simply by looking. Doing so may provide useful data, that rules some theories out, but more than one theory could be consistent with the data. How do we decide which theory is true, then? How do we know that anything is true? This is not an easy question to answer. Some observations may even be partly determined by the theories that we believe, so it is far from a simple matter in the scientific case. Truth in metaphysics is also hard work, but the point is that we shouldn't subject truth in metaphysics to any more stringent standards than we do in other cases. And what we probably then find is that our theories are provisional and fallible. We accept that they may have to be revised but that, nevertheless, it may be rational to work with them.

The relationship between metaphysics and science is likely to be a lot more complicated than the story just told. We often like the two to cohere even if they are not in outright conflict. Ideally, we would like a metaphysics that is fit for the world described by science, and science that is metaphysically sound. We have already seen a case that illustrates this. Questions were raised about simultaneity in Chapter 6: a notion that is challenged by relativity theory in science. Relativity theory does not refute certain philosophical accounts of absolute space and time, it could be maintained. But we may nevertheless think it preferable to develop a metaphysics for the way the world is, as described in the best available scientific theory. What we might then achieve is a scientifically informed metaphysics. This might give us a coherent account of the world that works on both a concrete and abstract level.

Theoretical virtues

In metaphysics, when deciding which account to hold, we have to look for a range of theoretical virtues. We look at how much of what really counts the theory can explain. Does it gel with our other theories to provide a unified account of the world? And does it explain much with very little, or are we assuming so much to get the theory started that its explanatory power is an illusion?

The theory that there are many other worlds, for example, has been recommended because it explains so much. It tells us what is possible, for instance. As we saw, however, for the theory to even get started, we had to assume the existence of each possibility at some real world. In that case, it looks like we only get out of the theory as explanation what we have put into it as assumption. We are thus often performing a balancing act whereby the number of assumptions is compared to explanatory power, like some sort of cosmic cost–benefit analysis.

Again, when we compare metaphysics to the search for knowledge in the sciences, it does not seem worlds apart. We want to find theories that explain the phenomena in a relatively simple way, requiring no outlandish assumptions or *ad hoc* hypotheses. For the sciences, the phenomena to be explained can include observational phenomena, such as the unexpected presence of a particle or movement of a planet. Such a movement would have to be entailed by the theory if that is to count as an explanatory success of it.

In metaphysics, the phenomena are not observational in the same way. We accept that some very abstract things have to be explained: there appears to be a plurality of particulars, for instance, and causation seems to be a feature of the world. How best to explain these general features? Once we explain what causation must be like in our world, we will then leave it to science to tell us what causes what. We just want to know what it is for one thing to cause another. And we adopt the same theoretical virtues as anyone else. We want to discover the best possible explanation of some feature of the world. It is just that the features that interest metaphysicists are abstract and very general. They cannot be observed in the way that you can observe a table or a cat, but perhaps they have been abstracted from what we have observed. We have a notion of particularity, from these things, and this is what we want to explain.

The value of metaphysics

It might seem that our critics have an argument that we cannot answer. We may have grounds for rejecting some theories and accepting others, provisionally, and in this respect, we may be offending no rational principle that anyone else would adopt, but the sheer uselessness of metaphysics shows why we shouldn't do it. Because science has at least some connection with the empirical world that we observe and with which we interact, we can use our scientific theories to get what we want. Science can be applied usefully. We can manipulate the world and use science to our own ends. Good science produces good results. Because metaphysics is so theoretical, so abstract, and so non-empirical, it seems that it has no pay-off at all. It doesn't allow us to manipulate the world around us. It is literally useless.

We need have no fear of this argument. In the first place, its basis is contestable. Causation, for instance, matters to everything. Our very manipulation of the world depends on causation. Nothing would make sense without it. And it turns out that we cannot know what causes what unless we have some theory – an inevitably metaphysical one – of what it is for something to cause something else. A philosophical misunderstanding could lead to a practical error, if we assumed causation was nothing more than correlation, for instance.

But suppose the basis of the argument is correct. Suppose metaphysics really is useful for nothing. Does this mean it is worthless? No. The value of many things is instrumental: they get you something else that you want. But some things have intrinsic value. They are valuable just for what they are, in their own right. Even if metaphysics is useless, its insights may be so deep and so profound that it could have the highest intrinsic value to us. It would give us a useless but deep understanding of the nature of reality. Indeed, Plato's idea makes sense. A metaphysical understanding of what the world is, how it works, and how it all fits together, in general and abstract terms, could be the most real and important thing there is. In that case, we don't do metaphysics so that we can stay healthy and wealthy: we want to stay healthy and wealthy so that we can do metaphysics.

Further reading

This book was intended as a very first read on the subject of metaphysics. If you are interested, what should you try next? A lot of material in philosophy is technical and should not be tackled lightly. In that case, I recommend moving next on to some of the lengthier and more involved introductions as an intermediate step. The following are all worth a try:

John Carroll and Ned Markosian, *An Introduction to Metaphysics* (Cambridge, 2010)
Jonathan Tallant, *Metaphysics: An Introduction* (Continuum, 2011)
Michael Jubien, *Contemporary Metaphysics: An Introduction* (Blackwell, 1997)
Michael Loux, *Metaphysics: A Contemporary Introduction* (Routledge, 2006)

In addition, there are plenty of books addressing the chapter topics of this book. Here are just a few that are particularly recommended, though they go beyond introductory level:

David Armstrong, *Nominalism and Realism* and *A Theory of Universals* (both Cambridge, 1978)
Joe Melia, *Modality* (Acumen, 2003)
Joshua Hoffman and Gary S. Rosenkrantz, *Substance: Its Nature and Existence* (Routledge, 1997)
Katherine Hawley, *How Things Persist* (Oxford, 2001)
Kathleen Wilkes, *Real People: Personal Identity without Thought Experiments* (Oxford, 1993)
Lawrence Lombard, *Events: A Metaphysical Study* (Routledge, 1986)

E. J. Lowe, *A Survey of Metaphysics* (Oxford, 2002) and *The Possibility of Metaphysics* (Oxford, 1998)

Phil Dowe, *Physical Causation* (Cambridge, 2000)

Robin Le Poidevin, *Travels in Four Dimensions* (Oxford, 2003)

Robin Le Poidevin, Peter Simons, Andrew McGonigal, and Ross Cameron, *The Routledge Companion to Metaphysics* (Routledge, 2009)

Stephen Mumford and Rani Lill Anjum, *Getting Causes from Powers* (Oxford, 2011)

Index

Logic
A Very Short Introduction
Graham Priest

Logic is often perceived as an esoteric subject, having little
to do with the rest of philosophy, and even less to do with real life.
In this lively and accessible introduction, Graham Priest shows
how wrong this conception is. He explores the philosophical
roots of the subject, explaining how modern formal logic deals
with issues ranging from the existence of God and the reality
of time to paradoxes of self-reference, change, and probability.
Along the way, the book explains the basic ideas of formal
logic in simple, non-technical terms, as well as the philosophical
pressures to which these have responded. This is a book for
anyone who has ever been puzzled by a piece of reasoning.

> 'a delightful and engaging introduction to the basic concepts of
> logic. Whilst not shirking the problems, Priest always manages to
> keep his discussion accessible and instructive.'

Adrian Moore, St Hugh's College, Oxford

> 'an excellent way to whet the appetite for logic.... Even if you read
> no other book on modern logic but this one, you will come away
> with a deeper and broader grasp of the *raison d'être* for logic.'

Chris Mortensen, University of Adelaide

www.oup.com/vsi